Mini Horse,
Mighty Hope

D1225434

Mini Horse, Mighty Hope

How a Herd of Miniature Horses Provides Comfort and Healing

Debbie Garcia-Bengochea
and Peggy Frezon

Revell
a division of Baker Publishing Group
Grand Rapids, Michigan

© 2021 by Debbie Garcia-Bengochea and Margaret S. Frezon

Published by Revell
a division of Baker Publishing Group
PO Box 6287, Grand Rapids, MI 49516-6287
www.revellbooks.com

Printed in the United States of America

Library of Congress Cataloging-in-Publication Data
Names: Garcia-Bengochea, Debbie, author. | Frezon, Peggy, 1961– author.
Title: Mini horse, mighty hope : how a herd of miniature horses provides comfort and healing / Debbie Garcia-Bengochea and Peggy Frezon.
Description: Grand Rapids, Michigan : Revell, a division of Baker Publishing Group, [2021]
Identifiers: LCCN 2021003885 | ISBN 9780800741273 (casebound) | ISBN 9780800739461 (paperback)
Subjects: LCSH: Miniature horses—Anecdotes.
Classification: LCC SF293.M56 G365 2021 | DDC 636.1/09—dc23
LC record available at https://lccn.loc.gov/2021003885

Published in association with Books & Such Literary Management, www.booksandsuch.com.

Some names and details have been changed to protect the privacy of the individuals involved.

To all of the children and adults who have been
loved by Gentle Carousel Miniature Therapy Horses
over the years, and to all of the volunteers who have
helped make this work possible.
—*Debbie Garcia-Bengochea*

To Sally and Gabriel, who introduced
me to the loving care of therapy animals.
And to Mike and our therapy dogs: to Ernest,
in memory of Ike, and to Pete (keep trying!).
And to Brooks, who set us on our mission of
rescuing senior dogs and inspired BrooksHaven.
—*Peggy Frezon*

Contents

1

"She watches through the window."

A moment can change every-thing. It happens in that snippet of time when you sit up and take notice. It happens in an instant that touches whatever comes before and transforms whatever comes after. There was such a moment when I realized miniature horses could change lives. That the beautiful spirit wrapped in flowing manes and pint-size hooves could touch hurting people and offer hope. And that moment came, literally, through an open door.

That humid morning in 1999, I stood on my neighbor's sun-bleached lawn beside my husband, Jorge, and a miniature bay horse no higher than my waist. Molly's full, black

9

mane ruffled in a stray breeze. She'd walked alongside us across our own little farm—a ranch-style house and barn on four acres outside of town—along the path beside the road, and up the neighbor's driveway to the front of a tidy ranch house much like our own. There Molly waited, ears pricked to the side, head lowered and relaxed. At seven years old, she was young and spry, yet as mellow as a sunny summer afternoon.

Jorge tapped on the front door. "We're here," he said.

Arthur, a tanned, older gentleman, came out to meet us. "I'm so grateful you could come," he said, glancing over at Molly and grinning. "Mama's going to be so happy." He led us to the side of the house and pointed to the front corner. "This is her window, here."

Earlier that week I'd been at the kitchen counter, detailing a lesson plan for my elementary school students, when Arthur had called. We knew Arthur well enough to stop and chat if we happened to be outside at the same time, but for the most part our conversations had been limited to polite inquiries about the weather and each other's health.

"Hot today," Arthur had begun. "How's everyone feeling?" Then he'd paused and said, "I, um, wonder if I might ask a favor? For Mama." I set down my pen and stepped away from the counter to focus on the request. I tried to picture our neighbor's mother—I knew the woman lived there but couldn't recall having met her.

"Yes, anything. Name it," I answered.

"You see," he continued, "she's getting up there . . . and, well, the doctor said they're doing all they can for her pain, but she could use something for her mind. Says we should try to get her involved, engaged in things. You see, she just lies there." His voice broke. "The only thing Mama seems interested in at all, to tell the truth, is your horses. She watches through the window. She can see out to your pasture from her bed."

A warmth spread over me at the thought of this man's mother finding joy in observing our little horses roaming about the field. When they played, full of life, maybe they made the frail, bedridden woman feel young and full of life too. Perhaps they helped her in the same way they helped me—horses had always brought me solace.

When I was young, I often felt like I was the skinny new girl whose military family moved too often and who was unsure of the trendiest way to style her long blonde locks or the popular clothes to wear. But not around horses. Now, even though I wore makeup and stylish outfits to work, in the barn I could dress comfortably and pull my hair back into a ponytail. The horses didn't seem to mind. They made me feel loved and accepted, just as they did when I was young. Seeing their slow, peaceful grazing in a field made my heart feel peaceful as well. So I could understand how Arthur's mother might feel while watching the horses through her window.

"I was just thinking . . . hoping . . . is there any way you'd consider walking one of your horses past Mama's window? So she could see it . . . up close?"

Of course we would. Such a small thing we could do to help.

So that morning I'd stepped into the barn bright and early, and paused before the stalls, deciding which horse to bring. There was Sugar, the first horse I'd ever owned. She was now a healthy and content old gal, but when we rescued her from the horse dealer she'd been a thin white pony with

11

dirty, shaggy fur and overgrown hooves. Jorge and I had taken one look at her and knew that she'd be coming home with us. We understood the plight that awaited an unwanted old horse in her condition. The moment I met her, I had a clear picture in my mind: I could see her clean and healthy, surrounded by happy children who talked to her and patted her while she gently nuzzled them back. Maybe this animal in need could help some children in need. And later she did, as boys and girls from my class came over to spend time

with her on the farm. While they patted and played with Sugar, I watched them relax and open up in a way I never saw in the classroom.

Then there was our miniature donkey, Bart, and two miniature horses, Molly and Misty. We found that, while some people may be intimidated by a large animal, most people felt secure with a miniature one. I chose Molly to visit Arthur's mom because she was so easygoing and cheerful. Also, her dark brown coat and flowing black mane would make her easier to see through the glass.

Arthur waved to attract his mother's attention. Jorge and I walked Molly across the lawn, back and forth in front of the window. She trotted along happily. I paused and looked to see if Mama had noticed. The little horse stretched on black-stockinged legs, arching her neck as if to see inside the window too.

12

The figure in the bed began to stir, lifting her head from the pillow and turning toward us. Her eyes widened and a warm smile spread across her face as she realized that one of the horses she had been watching from afar had come up close to say hello. She stretched a trembling hand toward us, as if to touch Molly. I swallowed hard and glanced at Jorge. Jorge looked from Molly to the front of the house and back. An introduction through the window just didn't feel like enough.

"You know," Jorge said, drawing out the words, unsure even as he spoke, "the front door is right there. Looks like the bedroom is pretty close."

"It is." Arthur pushed his glasses up on his nose. "It's just to the left."

A wooden wheelchair ramp spanned the front of the house. That was ideal—there were no stairs Molly would have to navigate. "Maybe we could open up the front door. Maybe Molly could poke her head in to say hello. What do you think?"

"Could you? Really?" Arthur's eyebrows raised.

At the time, there was no such thing as miniature therapy horses working indoors. Therapy dogs worked at nursing homes and maybe a few schools, but organized animal visitation for the purpose of bringing affection and emotional support was in its early stages. Dogs were restricted from most hospitals and public buildings. And horses? They remained outside, in stables and riding rings. Yet I knew that horses could have a positive effect on people. I saw it when my students came to the barn. I saw it when Jorge, who worked as a youth minister, invited families from church to visit. People relaxed, smiled. Even those who were usually anxious around animals felt safe with our minis. And students who were disruptive in class were instinctively calm and well behaved around the horses.

But Arthur's mother couldn't be brought to the horses. She couldn't get out of bed, much less the house. Arthur's only option was to bring a horse up close and hope that watching through the window would be enough to inspire his mother. Jorge and I wondered if we could go one step further to make their time together even more meaningful.

"You ready, girl?" Jorge asked as he led Molly to the front of the house. She had used ramps before to get into the trailer, so handling them now would be no problem. Her hooves tapped against the wooden slats. At the top we waited for Arthur to let us in. We were about to go through the open door. We were about to do something we'd never tried before.

Molly, Jorge, and I stood on the threshold. I could see into the room where Arthur's mother was lying in bed, her fragile frame swallowed by puffy linens. Arthur went ahead and helped her sit up, stuffing pillows behind her back. "We have a surprise for you," he said softly, pointing to the door. Molly peeked around the corner. Mama's hands fluttered to her cheeks and she let out a delighted cry. Cheerfulness bounced like a bubble from person to person, which seemed to encourage Arthur, because when he noticed how close the horse was, he unexpectedly pressed his weight against the wooden headboard. "Hang on!" he said, laughing, as he gently pushed the wheeled bed closer to the door. Once again, Jorge and I glanced at each other, exchanging an unspoken idea. *What if . . . ?*

Mama was close to the bedroom door now, and that was not far from the front door where we stood. A tan carpet covered the floor—a manageable, nonslip surface on which

Molly could walk. She seemed relaxed and content . . . yet she'd never been inside a house before. She had no kind of training for this. Any number of things could go wrong. Jorge whispered, "Is this really a good idea?" I cast a glance at the woman in bed. Someone in her condition could never travel to horses; they had to come to her. I nodded and took a deep breath.

Jorge took one step forward, Molly at his side. Then another. Mama turned toward us, a rosy blush rising on her cheeks. With twinkling eyes, she gazed at Molly. Even as Arthur's mother wanted to get to Molly, it looked as if the little horse wanted to reach her just as much. The two were connecting in some mysterious way. The same peace I felt when spending time with the horses in the barn settled around the room. Jorge moved Molly one step closer, until she was right alongside the bed. The woman's trembling hands found Molly's side, and her smile burst as she touched the horse for the first time. She slowly rubbed the horse's neck, down her nose, and under her chin. For a moment it seemed that all the dear woman's pain ceased and her worries disappeared. And in that space of time, life was sweet and hopeful.

Jorge and I let her linger in that moment, then led Molly back out the door and down the ramp. We made our way home, relieved that all went well and moved by the experience. I settled Molly into the pasture. "Well done," I said as Molly trotted off to find her pal, Misty.

That experience remained with me, planting itself firmly in my mind. Months later I ran into Arthur at the coffee shop downtown. He grinned and rushed over to talk to me, anxious to share his news. After Molly's visit, he explained, Mama had a breakthrough. She kept talking about

15

the horses. She developed a new, more positive outlook and became so motivated that she eventually got out of bed and into a chair. Of course, that chair was always pushed right up to the window to look out over the pasture. And later she even learned to use a walker and ventured outside where she could see and hear the horses from her yard. Her prognosis improved dramatically. "All thanks to Molly," Arthur said.

In the past we'd brought many people to visit the horses, but now a new idea was forming. *What if we brought horses inside to visit people? How many more people could we reach? Could such an idea really catch on?*

2

"When things get really bad, you've got to get really calm."

Step it up, Bart." I loosely held the lead line attached to the halter of our poky donkey and glanced up at the skies. There comes a time when either things are going to get better or they're going to get worse. And it looked like things were going to get worse.

If you live in southern Florida, you grow accustomed to storms, but that season of 2004 the hurricanes kept coming. First was Hurricane Charlie, making landfall with winds up to 150 mph. Our house survived, but Jorge and I spent long days pulling

17

heavy branches off the roof, lugging debris from the pasture, and patching holes in the barn. Hurricane Frances hit less than three weeks later, with lashing winds and drenching rains. The ground flooded and tree limbs tore down power lines. Two weeks later, we were just beginning to get things back together when forecasts reported that Hurricane Ivan was heading our way. And this one was expected to be even more powerful.

As part of the preparations, I was moving all our animals to a neighbor's stronger cement block barn. Previously, we'd made do with our own small wooden barn, but with so much damage already and strong winds picking up, we were taking no chances. I'd already brought Sugar, Molly, and Misty up the road. Bart was the last to go, but he was in no hurry. That was his nature. Or maybe he just didn't sense the urgency. What did a little donkey know about impending hurricanes? Maybe I'd been too casual. Jorge and I always said, "When things get really bad, you've got to get really calm." That's why I tended to the business at hand in an organized, steady manner. I'd tried not to project any anxiousness onto Bart. But couldn't he move a little faster?

We ambled down the street together at Bart's pace. I couldn't help glancing up at the clouds several times. They hung dark and heavy, and an eerie stillness filled the air. We'd been tracking the storm, and it was approaching fast. When we reached the barn, I waved to my neighbor in the distance—a slim woman in a nylon jacket who flitted about like a hummingbird on a row of hollyhocks. Like everyone, she was busy with her disaster plan, shuttering windows and securing outside objects.

I pushed open the barn's heavy sliding doors. Bart's hooves thumped against the planks, stirring up the sweet smell of pine shavings that covered the floor. I led him into a stall beside the others. Secretly, I wished I could have let him stay inside the house with us. Although he was pals with Molly and the other horses, Bart actually thought he was a dog. We had many house pets over the years, and Bart longed to be among them. Every day when I called the dogs inside, Bart appeared and lined up with them on the porch. When I opened the door, he cocked his head as if to say, *Can I come in too?* Sometimes I'd see him peeking inside the screen door, waiting optimistically. But he belonged in the pastures with plenty of room to roam and a nice cozy stall when it was cold or rainy. I scratched his ears and gave him some fresh hay. I filled the water buckets and made sure everyone was cozy, then got ready to leave. "Goodbye, Sugar. Goodbye, Molly." I paused at the door. I hated to go. "Be good, Bart."

For the rest of the day we kept informed of the weather forecasts and followed our well-practiced protocols. Before the storm hit, I decided to make one final trip into town for last-minute supplies. On my way down the long driveway, I spotted an unusual, reddish-brown animal out by the road, leaning against our gate. Drawing closer, I made out the shape of a dog. I rolled down the window and whistled. "Hey, fella, where do you belong?" He stirred and looked at me with deep, sad eyes. Hopefully he was just resting and would soon get up and head home.

I got out, opened the gate, and scratched the dog's head (trying unsuccessfully to avoid his mournful gaze) before getting back in the car. After I drove through and closed the gate, I called out, "Good boy. Now go on home where it's safe."

In town, I picked up the items on my list, scoured the near-empty shelves for more bottled water, tossed what I could in my cart, and paid. I returned from my errand and stopped to open the gate at the end of the driveway. There was the dog waiting for me. He hadn't budged.

He was medium sized, with short rusty fur and pert, pointy ears. He looked like a cattle dog, not uncommon in our area, yet I'd never seen him around before. When we made eye contact, he stood easily and took a step my way. Dust rose up from his unkempt fur, and upon closer inspection, I saw there was no collar around his neck. He let out one woof as if to say, *I've been waiting for you*. It was all I could do not to rush out and gather him into my arms.

"Don't you know a storm's coming?" If only I could have taken him into my car and gone door-to-door, searching the neighborhood to find where he lived. But there wasn't time. I pointed in a vague direction. "Get on home now. Hurry!" He wagged as I got out of the car to open the gate, but he didn't try to pass through, as if he was waiting for permission. *Polite*, I thought. He must belong to someone. I gave him a nice pat and encouraged him to move along. "Go home and be safe!"

"There's a dog out there," I told Jorge as I came through the door. "I know what you're thinking. We already have a houseful. We can't take in more. Besides, he's not ours." All the justification in the world did little to soothe my desire to rescue the dog. He must be hot. Hungry. Lonely. Scared.

Later, while fixing dinner, I looked out the window again. "Still there," I announced, my heart aching for him. He sat patiently leaning on the gate. I dawdled at the window, pretending to be busy but really just wanting to keep an eye on him.

Jorge came up behind me and gave me a gentle squeeze. "Whatcha waiting for?"

20

"What do you mean?" I asked.

"Well? Aren't you going to go get him?"

I spun around and ran out the door and down the driveway. The red dog rose to his feet at the sight of me and wagged furiously. This was the invitation he'd been waiting for. I opened the gate, and he jumped up and slapped his paws on my waist. I hugged him tight. "Okay, you win. Come on in. You're going to ride out the storm with us." He trotted beside me, tail wagging all the way to the house.

Late that evening, Hurricane Ivan hit. I secured the dogs— our new friend, along with our shaggy older dog Marcus—in crates for their safety. Our houseguest looked surprisingly relaxed, curled up on a quilt I'd slid inside to make him cozy. It was as if he'd known what he wanted back there at the gate—to be inside with the family he'd chosen. I was glad he was out of harm's way. We could wait until after the storm to find out where he belonged.

With flashlights at the ready, Jorge and I huddled in the middle of the house and turned on the radio. Rain pelted, slowly at first and then steadily increasing in intensity. Gales of wind shook the windows. I reminded myself how well prepared we were and all the measures we'd taken to secure the house. Before long the local stations were knocked out, and we listened to whatever we could get through the static. At every crash, I wondered what was happening outside. I thought about the horses up the road, and Bart, and our neighbors, and I prayed for their safety.

The storm roared on, like a freight train bearing down on us. Everything went dark. We were in the worst of it now. The house shook. The roof sounded as if it was being ripped apart tile by tile. There was nothing we could do but

21

wait. When the clamor died down, I realized that I'd been holding my breath and let it out in a great rush. As the air escaped, I felt as if all the energy left my body too, and there was no strength left to haul myself to my feet. I rubbed my

tingling arms and sat in the dark, wondering if it was over or if there was more to come. With the house boarded up tight, there was no way to see anything outside. So we just waited some more.

Daybreak came. The morning hung eerily quiet. Even without knowing the extent of the damage, I felt awash with gratitude. "We're safe," I said.

Jorge got up and leaned hard against the back door, trying to push it open, but it was blocked by some kind of debris. A branch? A tree? The barn? Together we got the door open, forcing aside what turned out to be piles of rubble. I rubbed my eyes—nothing looked the same. It was as if we were in *The Wizard of Oz* and the house had been lifted up and set back down in a whole new location. Fallen trees covered the yard. Wreckage littered the ground. Someone's patio furniture rested against a broken fence. Huge gashes split the siding and trees tottered on the roof. One look at the devastation renewed my respect for the formidable power of nature. The entire yard was flooded. "Look!" I said, pointing. Little brown fish swam past our feet.

A few days later Jorge presented me with an even more unsettling report. The hurricane had carried an alligator into our pond. "It's still small," Jorge said, "about three and a half feet long."

"What do we do about it?" I asked.

"Fish and Game said we can't touch it. It's protected."

"Okay, *we* can't move it. But can someone come get it?"

"It's not large enough to be legally removed."

"So, what now? We live with this alligator in the pond?"

"I guess we wait until he gets bigger. Or maybe he'll leave on his own."

Wearing my high boots, I carefully trudged over near the pond to take a look. Two partially submerged eyes stared back at me. I cast a skeptical glance. The alligator seemed quite content there.

Eventually, we learned that Ivan was a Category 5 storm, the strongest intensity hurricane to make landfall. Winds had gusted up to 165 mph. The storm surge peaked at around fifteen feet. Boats were stacked in marinas and even carried far inland. A subdivision twenty miles from the coast was destroyed. More than a million people were without electricity. There were 123 fatalities. How could anyone ever get used to those types of statistics?

As soon as the water receded enough, we retrieved the horses from our neighbor's barn. Jorge and I pulled on our tall rubber boots to protect ourselves from dangerous water moccasins and navigated our way up the street. We knew well enough not to step in standing water—if any puddle had come in contact with a downed power line, the action could prove fatal. The entire path was pummeled with devastating destruction—we passed massive palm fronds littering the ground, a demolished orange grove, and telephone poles snapped in half.

Once we got Bart and the horses back, I sat on a bench near the stalls and tried to find my bearings. The barn always drew me whenever I needed peace. Whenever my schedule was too demanding. Whenever a student required extra attention and I needed to figure out the best way to help. Whenever family problems grew overwhelming. I'd go to the barn and sit there among the horses—just as I did that day after the hurricane.

I rubbed Misty's velvety ears, and she leaned into me tenderly. The muscles in my forehead relaxed. I hadn't even realized how much stress I'd been lugging around until I sensed it slowly dissipating. My heart rate calmed. This was the comfort the horses offered. This was why I felt so strongly about getting them out to reach others. I wanted everyone to be able to experience that feeling. Instead of bringing school kids to us, we'd begun visiting schools. We'd even taken the first carefully planned steps inside certain places.

So many people needed the hope.

I needed the hope.

I offered Misty a treat and felt her lips rub against my hand, like being kissed by a man with a mustache. I stayed there patting the horses for hours. Everything was going to be okay. The work of recovery would be slow, but we *would* recover.

3

"He needed a home."

Cleaning up the hurricane damage challenged our minds and muscles, but we were getting it done. I felt lucky, while at the same time I ached for all the people who had lost homes, lost loved ones, or lost everything. The newspaper was packed with listings of items and animals for sale by people who had salvaged belongings but had no place to keep them.

"We need to replace some equipment," I said. "Maybe if we get what we need at one of these auctions, we could help someone out."

Jorge stayed home to work on repairs while I drove three hours, the sides of the road littered with debris, to the nearest auction house. Walking past harnesses, buckets, and blankets, I stopped at a pen of miniature horses. I hadn't intended to look, but one caught my eye—jet black, tiny, very sweet and mellow.

A woman with a folder of papers tucked under her arm approached. "He's cute, huh? Do you like him? Are you looking for a horse?"

"Oh no. No, no, not today." I tried to ignore the sweetness of the little nose nuzzling me through the wire.

"This would be a good time to get yourself a little friend." The woman smiled gently, her expression sincere. "The foals are still young. They won't go for much, I'm sure." Her voice wavered. "If you were at all interested . . . we're in a bad way. Our barn was destroyed, and we've got no place for them now. We hate to, but we have to let them go."

My gaze shifted from the woman's sad eyes to the horse's eyes, sparkling with friendliness. "I wish I could help. I'll have to think about it," I said, my own voice a bit shaky. Another horse, however cute, wasn't in our plans.

"Tell you what, if you don't get one during the auction, check back with me after. I'll make you a good deal on what's left." She started off, then paused and implored over her shoulder, "We can't take them back. We've got nothing."

I felt sorry for the woman. And the horses were cute. It would be nice having a little foal to watch grow up. I smiled at the one that had caught my eye, imagined him in our barn and romping across our fields. Was this really an offer too good to refuse?

A young girl in a wheelchair rolled up by my side. "Look, Grammy, look!" she said as her grandmother squeezed in between us. The girl's face lit up with a huge smile. She bobbed in the wheelchair, pumping her slender arms in delight.

"My, aren't they pretty?" the older woman said and then turned to me. "I'm sorry . . . my granddaughter is excited."

"I can see that. The students in my school react the same way when they get near a miniature horse. Especially adorable ones like these."

"Oh, are you a teacher?"

"Yes. Some of the children I teach have disabilities. We like to bring them back to our barn to meet the horses whenever we can. And we've started taking the horses places to visit children, and adults too—those who are ill, those who can't get out. We've worked hard to train the horses so they'll feel safe and comfortable stepping inside a building. It's been a slow process, but it's also been amazing. The horses seem to reach people in a special way. It's been quite something to see."

"That's wonderful. What a blessing you are to those kids."

"Looks like you have your own blessing." I nodded toward the little girl, who couldn't keep her eyes off the animals playing in the pen.

"Oh yes. Today we're looking for a special horse for my granddaughter."

"I'm sure you'll find her just the right companion." I smiled, confident that a little horse would be able to help this child through whatever might lie ahead. I knew what a powerful bond could exist between a girl and a horse.

When I was young, I thought of horses constantly—I read every horse book I could find, collected toy model horses, and doodled pictures of horses around the edges of my school binder. In my deepest imaginings I dreamt about owning

27

a horse, but I knew it was impossible. My military family moved—from Texas, to Colorado, to Washington, to New Jersey—at least once a year. There was no way I could keep a

horse if we never stayed in one place. Instead, I always managed to find a stable nearby or to persuade some sympathetic rancher to let me muck stalls and pitch hay in exchange for riding lessons. I worked hard just to be near the animals I loved so much.

The horses were my very best friends. My father was often away serving our country. My mother was busy managing the family by herself. And friendships were fleeting. I'd start a new school, make a friend, only to move, leave the school, and lose my friend. *Don't get close to people*, I reminded my young self, *because you're just going to leave.* I thought of all the times I'd tiptoed into the stable and sat on a bale of hay and said, "No one understands." The horses listened. I whispered in their ears, and they nuzzled their velvety noses against my cheek. I knew they comprehended my every word. They cared. They understood.

A bell rang to signal the start of the auction, so I took my seat. The items moved swiftly, and I bid on some supplies we needed. Then bidding started on the horses. First a bay. Then a lovely white filly. The tiny, jet-black foal was up next, and suddenly I knew I wanted that horse more than anything. He needed a home, and we had space for him. He was adorable and so small that I could take him home in the

28

back of the minivan. I couldn't shake the feeling that he was meant for me.

My hand shot up. The auctioneer acknowledged me. Then came another bid. It's not that I expected to be the only one in the running, but it startled me. I turned my head to see who had bid. It was the grandmother with the little girl in the wheelchair. We were vying for the same horse. The auctioneer returned to me, and I nodded automatically. But when the grandmother bid again, I took one look at the little girl and set my number down on my lap. The auctioneer glanced at me again. I caught the grandmother's attention and smiled. I couldn't bid anymore, not against a little girl who needed a horse for a friend just like I had when I was young. The grandmother smiled back and raised her number. A few others joined in, but in the end the grandmother won. I let out a grateful sigh.

After the auction, I met up with the woman and the girl near the exit. "Congratulations," I said. "Your granddaughter is going to love that little horse."

The woman smiled warmly, a twinkle in her eye. "Oh no. My granddaughter decided on a different horse."

I paused, confused. "She did?"

The woman smiled wider and pressed a paper into my hand. "She wanted this one for you."

"But . . ." I protested.

"We insist. He belongs with you. He'll help many kids in need. We want to do this." The granddaughter beamed and nodded.

Shocked, I hugged them both. "Thank you so much!" I turned to stroke the tiny foal in the pen. He was mine after all. When I turned back, the woman and her granddaughter

29

were gone. I scanned the crowd, but I didn't see them anywhere. I never learned the names of the mysterious grandmother and granddaughter who appeared like angels and gave me such a remarkable gift.

A baby miniature horse is tiny, but I wanted to be sure to get him loaded into my vehicle safely and securely. I lined the back of the van with some hay and lifted him gently. The little guy was so young, I didn't want to frighten him. I got into the driver's seat and whispered and sang to him all the way home.

When I pulled up to the house, Jorge was outside repairing a broken fence rail. "Can you help me get something out of the van?" I asked.

Jorge tilted his head as he looked over. "What did you do?" He set down his tools and opened the back of the van. Two bright eyes looked back at him. "Debbie! How did this happen?" he asked. Yet I knew his heart for helping animals was as big as mine.

"He needed a home," I said simply. And we both fell in love.

Now we had a new horse to care for, but we still had to figure out what to do about the gentle, red cattle dog. We'd taken him to the vet and had him scanned for a microchip, but he had none. We'd put a notice in the paper and online, hung signs and posted pictures, but no one claimed him. One day he was sprawled out on our living room armchair. "It doesn't matter that he was lost, or there was a hurricane, or that he's here in new surroundings, he's happy as a lark," Jorge said. We never found out where he came from, but Lark had found his family.

It's impossible to say anything good about a tragedy. There is nothing positive in the loss of lives and the destruction of homes. Hurricane Ivan wreaked havoc across the state of Florida and beyond. The cleanup and restoration cost billions. Although we were blessed—our home and barn were spared—the hurricane had been devastating; we were without power and had mountains of work and cleanup ahead. But it never ceases to amaze me the way animals come into my life. The hurricane had brought us a horse and a dog . . . and eventually, even the alligator grew on me.

4

"Your horses smell like flowers."

We named the little black foal from the auction Sparkle. He was the third miniature horse to join our family. After that, the herd grew like daisies in a field. We'd come so far since stepping foot (and hoof) inside Arthur's house. I felt a pull to bring the horses to people who needed their comfort and love—people who couldn't get out to see the horses. We'd started small, by visiting local schools. Inevitably, a teacher or parent would ask if there was any way we could stop by and say hello to someone they knew, someone sick or in need. We visited nursing homes, and after years of training, our horses began

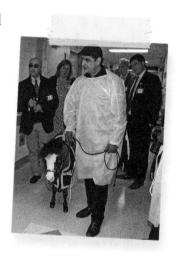

working in hospitals too. Each time, we saw how people were encouraged by interacting with a living creature who accepted them and gave them unconditional love. Maybe it was because the horses seemed to listen and didn't try to fix them. Whatever it was, we sensed that we were onto something that people needed. Word spread and our schedule filled with requests.

We moved to a larger farm with plenty of room for the horses to roam. We even gave ourselves a real, official name. One evening after dinner, Jorge had been doing some paperwork at the dining room table as I was penciling in dates on the calendar. He suddenly looked up and said, "We should have a name."

It hadn't occurred to me before, but he made a good point. "What should it be?" We ran through ideas. *Mini Hooves. Helping Hooves. Hooves and Hearts.* Nothing felt right. "Let's think of something young people can relate to. Something fun." We went back and forth, exchanging ideas. Parties, ice cream, toys, parades, games.

"Merry-go-rounds?" Jorge suggested.

I looked up. "Yes! Because of the little horses on the ride. But not merry-go-round . . . it should be carousel. Hmmm . . . what about Miniature Carousel? Or Happy Carousel?" I rubbed my chin. Close but not quite.

The people we visited were often ill or hurting. Fragile. They needed to be approached gently. And our horses were always so very gentle. "*Gentle* Carousel," I said. Jorge's smile reflected my own. It felt right.

So, after eight years of serving families, Gentle Carousel became an official nonprofit organization in 2008. Even so, the idea of therapy horses in houses and places of business was still new, and not everyone felt comfortable allowing them inside.

It felt like a positive sign when the prestigious medical school at Columbia University invited us to speak on the topic of therapy horses. That brisk November, Jorge and I drove the horse trailer all the way up to New York City. Magic was going to college! The students were interested and eager to learn, and we felt like we were sharing an important message. Our presence also attracted a great deal of media attention.

One day while we were in New York, I received a call from Dr. Elizabeth Mann at the nearby Mount Sinai Hospital. She told us about one of her patients who was in palliative care in the ICU and might not have long to live. "She has no family," the doctor with the kind voice said. "I asked her if I could get her anything, if she had any wishes. She used to be a horseback rider, and she said, 'I just want to lie in a pasture filled with horses.'" Dr. Mann explained that she had wondered how to make this wish come true at a hospital in the middle of Manhattan, but when she heard on the news that we were in town, it seemed like a miraculous answer. "I was just hoping," she said, "would you come?"

We would.

The next morning, Jorge and I walked Magic into the van and set off for the hospital. While we were on the way, driving down the jam-packed city streets, the phone rang again. Dr. Mann told us that she wasn't sure if it was going to work out because there were some concerns about allowing a horse in the ICU. The doctor told us to keep coming while she tried to work things out.

I hung up the phone and shook my head. I wanted to be there for this woman. Our horses were experienced working in hospitals and intensive care units, and we took careful precautions to make sure they were healthy, clean, and safe. Every morning we woke up bright and early and went out to the penned enclosure around the barn where the horses slept. Although they are trained to work inside, it is important to us that they live outside and lead a natural life. Like wild horses, our miniatures have all bonded to create a herd. They know where they stand in the pecking order and defer to the leader, a mare named Wakanda, who can direct them with a whinny or a subtle flick of her ear. They have fifteen acres of land to explore and the freedom to make their own choices—when to eat, where to run, whether to roll in the sand or take a nap. That makes happier horses, which makes better therapy animals.

Before every event, the horses working that day are bathed and groomed. Once, a young girl buried her face deep into one horse's soft, flowing mane and came up smiling. "Your horses smell like flowers," she said. That became our goal for every visit—that the tiny horses would always smell like flowers. So that day before heading to Mount Sinai Hospital, we'd bathed and groomed Magic at the farm where we were staying, and she was clean and neat and smelled like a fresh bouquet of roses.

When we arrived at the hospital, everything was a go after all. We brought Magic up the elevator to the intensive care unit. As the elevator doors parted, everyone standing in the hall did a double take. They pointed and broke into broad smiles. They never expected to see a horse stepping off the elevator. Dr. Mann met us and thanked us for coming. She had us slip into gowns and bright blue rubber gloves before entering the ICU.

"Terry, look who came to see you," the doctor said, gesturing for us to move closer. I could clearly see the toll that illness had taken in the woman's gaunt features, yet she turned her head expectantly toward us. Magic slowly walked in the door and, as if sizing up the situation, quickened her pace to Terry's bedside.

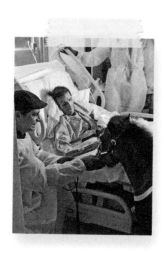

"Ohhhh! What a beautiful horse," Terry said, her face lighting up. Magic moved close and settled her head down on the bed. Nothing we did prompted Magic to do this—she just seemed to want to get near and felt that it would comfort the woman. Terry reached out her thin arm and patted Magic's nose. "Hello, sweetie. Hello, girl." The woman was clearly comfortable around a horse, and Magic enjoyed the attention. Terry rubbed Magic's ears. "Do you like your ears rubbed?"

Jorge nodded. "She does. It's her favorite spot."

Terry stroked the horse, keeping her gaze on Magic's bright, blue eyes. At times she looked as if she was in a faraway place. Then she closed her eyes and smiled.

I stood respectfully aside. During most of our visits, Jorge and I and the volunteers wear black and try to fade into the background. We don't want the limelight. Such moments are all about the patient and the horse.

Doctors and nurses who had been caring for Terry over her lengthy stay filtered into the room. I could tell they cared about this woman, as they became choked up watching her. "Uh, it must be dusty in here," an intern said, wiping the tears from his eyes and trying to pretend he wasn't emotional.

A large group of staff and administrators gathered as we made our way out. "I'm so impressed," a man in a suit said. "This went so beautifully, and it meant so much. And to think, it almost didn't happen."

We heard that Terry passed away soon after, her last wish fulfilled. All I could hope was that her beautiful soul was resting among a whole field of horses.

No matter where we go or what we are doing, we hear about someone in need, someone like Terry. That's why whenever we are in any town for any event, we arrange to stop at a nearby hospital, nursing home, or school. We travel often, and our schedule is packed, but we are always willing to try to squeeze in one more visit. And that one visit could be what brightens someone's day, helps them forget the pain for a while, or gives them affection and comfort on a really bad day—it could be the one thing they need most at that moment.

When we returned from New York, I let Magic out to the pasture, and she ran to greet the rest of the herd. We'd lost our senior horses, Molly and Sugar, but also added many new horses over the years. They raced in a wide circle, little legs beating and kicking the air, thick manes flowing. They slowed to a walk, following each other, then divided into little groups and grazed. I leaned contentedly against the trailer and watched our beautiful little herd. Each one was special.

Meet the Horses

ALADDIN

Gender: Gelding

Significance of name: Named after a favorite children's story character who is independent, clever, and kindhearted.

Appearance: White with bright blue eyes.

Personality: Loyal; dependable in challenging situations.

Therapy work: Aladdin works in hospitals, hospices, and assisted living programs. He's a favorite at schools and literacy events. He was with the first team of therapy horses to work at Sandy Hook in Newtown, Connecticut. As one of the Santa Ponies, he attends many holiday events and is calm on large concert stages.

Mini tidbit: Aladdin likes to stand under his favorite tree with his friends.

AMAZING GRACE

Gender: Mare

Significance of name: Grace was born while the therapy horses were working in Charleston, South Carolina, after the tragic shooting at Emanuel AME Church. The Charleston residents suggested the name to reflect their hope and faith.

Appearance: Sorrel with a bald face, three long white stockings, and big blue eyes.

Personality: Very social. She is every other horse's best friend.

Therapy work: Grace works with adults and children in hospital care and with families of first responders.

Mini tidbit: Amazing Grace is very athletic and loves to jump.

ANTHEM

Gender: Gelding

Significance of name: At the time Anthem was born, the horses were starting to spend a lot of time in Nashville, so we chose a musical name for him.

Appearance: White with black markings. His face is all white, and his ears are white on the outside but black on the inside. Because of this, some children think he looks like a toy.

Personality: Fearless and trusting.

Therapy work: Anthem works at Ronald McDonald Houses. He also works with young patients and adults at rehab hospitals. Anthem often makes school visits.

Mini tidbit: Anthem is a movie star! He had a mini part as the character Light in the film *Apple of My Eye*, which stars Burt Reynolds and Amy Smart.

BART, The Miniature Donkey

Gender: Jack

Significance of name: Named after a man who helped out on the farm many years ago.

Appearance: Gray with a black cross on his back and big, soft brown eyes.

Personality: Kind and protective of his equine friends. Can be a bit stubborn. He lives with the herd of therapy horses.

Therapy work: Bart sometimes works in schools and libraries. Children think he looks like Eeyore or the title character in the book *Brighty of the Grand Canyon* by Marguerite Henry.

Mini tidbit: He can walk so quietly, he sometimes sneaks up on people!

CIRCUS

Gender: Gelding

Significance of name: Circus was already named when he arrived as a foal. His nickname is Polka Dot (or just Pokey).

Appearance: White with black spots all over. He looks like a Dalmatian.

Personality: Gentle and easygoing.

Therapy work: Circus works at schools, libraries, and hospitals. He helps children with his "You Have Been Spotted Being Kind" anti-bullying/pro-kindness program.

Mini tidbit: He loves food and has to work hard to stay at a healthy weight. He likes taking long naps.

CLOUDBURST

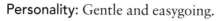

Gender: Gelding

Significance of name: His mom's name is Stormy Weather, so we thought that a little Cloudburst seemed fitting.

Appearance: Chestnut pinto with bright blue eyes.

Personality: Bossy, take-charge, and wants to be involved in everything.

Therapy work: Cloudburst enjoys working in hospitals, Ronald McDonald Houses, hospice programs, assisted living programs, schools, libraries, and book and literacy festivals.

Mini tidbit: He once worked at a dance-a-thon for the Children's Miracle Network.

DREAM

Gender: Mare

Significance of name: She was so sweet, she seemed like a dream come true.

Appearance: A beautiful pinto with a very long white tail and a fluffy white mane that children love.

Personality: Quiet; never pushy. She always waits her turn.

Therapy work: Dream works with patients in hospitals and hospice care and with military families.

Mini tidbit: She is usually the first horse to run in from the pasture to get attention. She loves spending time with people.

MAGIC

Gender: Mare

Significance of name: Magic was named before coming to Gentle Carousel as a foal, but we got lucky because the name is absolutely perfect.

Appearance: Jet black with a wide blaze and striking bright blue eyes.

Personality: Capable, steady, empathetic.

Therapy work: Magic visits hospitals, hospices, assisted living facilities, schools, libraries, and Ronald McDonald Houses. She has a literacy program called "Reading Is Magic." She has comforted people after tragedies at Sandy Hook Elementary School in Newtown, Connecticut; Emanuel AME Church in Charleston, South Carolina; and Pulse nightclub in Orlando, Florida. She traveled to Moore, Oklahoma, to help out after tornadoes devastated the town.

Mini tidbit: Magic always finds the person in the room who needs her most. She's also been featured in many books, including *The Dog in the Dentist Chair* by Peggy Frezon, *Book of Heroes* by National Geographic, *Animal Superheroes* by Scholastic Books, and *Heroic Animals* by Clare Balding.

44

MERCURY

Gender: Gelding

Significance of name: Thousands of people sent in name ideas for Mercury. Children in hospital care selected his name from our top-three favorites. They chose the name because he runs fast, like the Roman god Mercury.

Appearance: Smoky black and white, with one white ear and one dark ear, three white legs and one dark leg, and a tail that is half black and half white.

Personality: Busy, active. He runs and leaps and has boundless energy.

Therapy work: Mercury enjoys visiting literacy programs at schools and libraries with his dog pal, Sirius. He also visits children's hospitals.

Mini tidbit: From the day he was born, Mercury became best pals with Sirius, our Maremma sheepdog puppy. They even have similar markings. They are both featured in Debbie's book *Mercury and Sirius*.

MISTY

Gender: Mare

Significance of name: Named after the title character from the popular children's book *Misty of Chincoteague* by Marguerite Henry.

Appearance: White with blue eyes and a big patch of color over one eye.

Personality: Intelligent and patient, particularly with youngsters.

Therapy work: Misty enjoys meeting young readers at literacy programs inside schools and libraries.

Mini tidbit: She enjoys being pampered. She likes to get a back massage after her bath.

MOONSHADOW

Gender: Mare

Significance of name: She was born on the first day of spring during a supermoon.

Appearance: Smoky black with swirly markings that look like the Milky Way, with a perfectly shaped star on her shoulder.

Personality: Energetic and fearless.

Therapy work: Tiny Moonshadow is popular with older adults in assisted living programs and with children at reading programs. She visits veterans and children's hospitals.

Mini tidbit: She's been a guest at popular equestrian events and once made her entrance riding inside a convertible! A character named Moonshadow in the book *High Paw, Super Sebastian!* by Jasmine Cabanaw is based on Moonshadow.

PRINCE

Gender: Gelding

Significance of name: He was born on the same day as Prince George, the son of Prince William and Kate Middleton of England.

Appearance: Prince weighed only six pounds when he was born. He is white with blue eyes. Children think he looks like a unicorn.

Personality: Strong, with unlimited energy.

Therapy work: Prince is a natural in children's hospitals and at literacy programs.

Mini tidbit: He appeared onstage at the famous Franklin Theatre in Nashville, Tennessee.

RAINBOW

Gender: Gelding

Significance of name: We picked the name because sighting a rainbow is a promise of good things to come.

Appearance: Dapple-gray pinto with dark patches around his eyes that make his face look like a panda's. He is one of the smallest horses in the herd.

Personality: Determined and fearless. Trustworthy with even the most fragile patients.

Therapy work: Rainbow works at hospitals, libraries, and schools. He is extra careful with children who have disabilities.

Mini tidbit: When he was a foal, he met canine movie superstar Benji.

SCOUT

Gender: Gelding

Significance of name: He is curious, likes to explore, and enjoys adventures.

Appearance: Pinto with a long mane and an extra-long tail that is half black and half white, and bright blue eyes. He is one of the smallest horses in the herd.

Personality: Very active, fearless. He enjoys going on hikes.

Therapy work: Scout works with veterans and children with disabilities. He is also a Junior Ranger for the Florida State Parks.

Mini tidbit: He has been kissed by country music legend Barbara Mandrell! His mother is therapy horse Wakanda.

SNOW ANGEL

Gender: Mare

Significance of name: Named because she was born on a rare day when it snowed on the farm in Florida. She is also white like snow.

Appearance: Medicine Hat—a unique color pattern of a mostly white body with a little color on the ears and top of the head that resembles a bonnet or hat.

Personality: Active when playing, yet calm and gentle when working.

Therapy work: Angel is part of a team of white horses we call the Hospital Angels.

Mini tidbit: She has two look-alike full siblings, Sweetheart and Takoda.

SPARKLE

Gender: Gelding

Significance of name: Named for the way his eyes sparkle.

Appearance: Blue roan. He looked solid black as a foal and has matured to a lighter shade with spots and a black mane and tail.

Personality: Friendly and mellow.

Therapy work: Sparkle works in hospitals, literacy programs, and anti-bullying/pro-kindness programs. He is a favorite in schools.

Mini tidbit: He has been best friends with Circus since they were foals—almost sixteen years! They both have spots.

SUNDANCE

Gender: Gelding

Significance of name: A sun dance is a Native American ceremony. His nickname is Sunny.

Appearance: Buckskin

Personality: Wonderfully kind and loving.

Therapy work: Sundance is often seen at literacy programs. He has worked with foster children and many children with autism.

Mini tidbit: Sundance is a rescue horse. A character based on Sundance is featured in a book about foster children called *Jason and Elihu* by Shelley Fraser Mickle. Sundance autographs books by kissing a page that features his photo.

SUNSHINE

Gender: Mare

Significance of name: Named for her sweet, happy personality.

Appearance: Sorrel with white markings. Her bright blue eyes are the first thing people notice about her.

Personality: Happy, friendly, and loves attention.

Therapy work: Sunshine works at hospitals, libraries, and many community events.

Mini tidbit: She is always at the pasture gate waiting for her turn to be groomed. She loves to be brushed . . . the longer the better.

SWEETHEART

Gender: Mare

Significance of name: In addition to having a sweet

51

personality, she has three heart-shaped markings on her side.

Appearance: Medicine Hat—a unique pattern of a mostly white body with color on the ears and top of the head that resembles a bonnet or hat.

Personality: Sweet and gentle.

Therapy work: Sweetheart works at hospitals, hospice programs, and libraries. She loves doing programs with Santa Claus as part of a team of white horses we call the Hospital Angels.

Mini tidbit: She loves to follow people around the farm and always wants to be the one to go on a visit. She has look-alike full siblings, Snow Angel and Takoda.

TAKODA

Gender: Gelding

Significance of name: Takoda is a Native American name that means "friend to everyone."

Appearance: Medicine Hat—a unique pattern of mostly white body with color on the ears and top of the head that resembles a bonnet or hat.

Personality: Friendly, active, and gentle.

Therapy work: Takoda works in hospitals and schools. He's part of a team of white horses we call the Hospital Angels.

Mini tidbit: He needs a lot of exercise and loves to run around our many acres of pasture. He has look-alike sisters, Snow Angel and Sweetheart. They are his full siblings, each a few years apart in age.

TOBY

Gender: Gelding

Significance of name: He was born while the therapy horses were working with tornado survivors in Moore, Oklahoma. The children of Moore named him after Toby Keith, the popular Oklahoma-born country singer, who grew up in Moore.

Appearance: Sorrel with a thick *Lion King* mane and big brown eyes.

Personality: Strong and courageous.

Therapy work: Toby works at hospitals and Ronald McDonald Houses. He also visits families who have experienced traumatic events.

Mini tidbit: He is a survivor. He had major surgery when he was a few weeks old, and his exercise had to be limited for a long time. He's now healthy and active. Young patients can relate to Toby when they hear that he, too, spent time in a hospital when he was young.

53

WAKANDA

Gender: Mare

Significance of name: Wakanda is a Native American name that means "possesses magical powers."

Appearance: Chestnut pinto, with one brown eye and one blue eye.

Personality: Dependable and friendly.

Therapy work: Wakanda can be found in hospitals, hospice programs, assisted living homes, libraries, and schools. She comforted people after the tragedy at Sandy Hook Elementary School in Newtown, Connecticut, and after tornadoes struck Moore, Oklahoma.

Mini tidbit: She is the leader of the therapy horse herd, and all the other horses defer to her wishes. She's also the mother of Scout and Moonshadow.

5

"Shake it off."

Rainbow, our miniature dapple-gray horse, stood on the polished linoleum of the hospital hallway. Doctors in scrubs and nurses with clipboards stared. Hospital techs pushing gurneys smiled. They all paused from their work, pulled out their cell phones, and began snapping pictures like paparazzi.

We visit hospitals nearly every week and have found many ways the horses can help patients. If a child is refusing treatments, often the horse's presence is enough to encourage them to give it a try. Sometimes we join physical therapy sessions, keeping pace beside a patient who is relearning how to walk. Other times we visit the burn unit. Once, we stopped in to see a sweet child who was in tears at the grueling tasks ahead of her—a long rehabilitation and painful exercises for her badly burned arms. Many young girls love to brush and braid the horses' manes, so I thought maybe we could reach her in this way. "Would you like to help groom our horse?" I asked. I offered her a child-sized, sparkly pink brush that I keep with our supplies. She accepted, and before long she was carefully brushing Dream's mane, never realizing that her movements were actually part of her physical therapy. Having the horse there that day made a difference.

We often visit children who have experienced traumatic brain injuries or have life-threatening diseases. On this day when people in the halls were taking pictures of Rainbow like paparazzi, we hoped to cheer children in the pediatric oncology unit. Because days are full of challenges for children battling cancer, we want our visits to be fun and special—more than just having someone poke their head in the door and say hi. The time spent with one of our horses might be a once-in-a-lifetime experience, so it should be extra special. I try to come up with creative touches that will amuse the children, like decorating the horses' manes and tails with glittery sparkles. "It's fairy dust," I tell them, and they look back at me with wonder and crowd in line to pat the horses and get the enchanted fairy dust all over their hands.

I remember one time when a young boy had been particularly delighted with Magic and the sparkly glitter he got on his fingertips. So later I was confused when I saw the boy sitting alone, arms wrapped around his knees, tears running down his cheeks.

"What's the matter?" I asked.

"The doctor made me wash it off." He showed me his freshly scrubbed hands.

Although I knew the doctor had a good reason for wanting this boy's hands shiny clean, I ached for the child. Magic, however, knew just what to do. She edged closer to the young boy until they were face-to-face. The boy leaned in and rested his forehead against hers, a way of connecting that many people feel drawn to do, a touch that seems especially healing. When Magic moved back, I broke into a wide grin. Some of the glitter had rubbed off from her mane, and fairy dust sprinkled the boy's nose.

I wished that same kind of magical encounter for the young patients in the oncology unit that day. Rainbow was ready to do his best to cheer them up. Our dedicated volunteers stood by to offer their invaluable assistance, as they do everywhere we go. One of them carried a basket brimming with stuffed horses—we always leave one on each child's bed as a tangible reminder of the happy visit. The hospital staff member who was with us that day told us that everyone was ready. Each of our horses has their own theme song, so I scrolled through my iPod and cued up Rainbow's track: "Somewhere Over the Rainbow." I pushed the play button, and the little gray horse swished his long tail, ready to work.

The staff member led us all through a set of heavy double doors. As they heard the familiar tune and the tip-tapping of Rainbow's little hooves, some of the children peeked out of their rooms, clapping and laughing to see a tiny horse in the hall.

In the first room we entered, a girl with rosy cheeks and a kerchief on her head sat waiting for us in a wheelchair. Pillows and teddy bears lined her bed, and rows of greeting cards and photographs decorated her wall, giving me the impression that she'd been in the hospital a long while. Her face lit up as we approached.

"This is Rainbow," I said. "He's here to spend some time with you."

The girl nodded, wide-eyed. "I knew I'd meet a pony today," she said. I marveled at her sincerity. It seemed that children were often able to believe something unexpected and wonderful was right around the corner. That was another

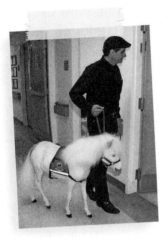

reason we worked so hard to make our events special—so that when we walked into a room, a pretty little horse might bring a smile to an ill child's face and help create a reprieve from the pain and the challenging hospital routine.

She reached out and stroked Rainbow. For one so young, she had such a gentle and loving touch. Rainbow stretched his neck over the arm of the wheelchair. I thought about what kind of experience might be extra meaningful to this child. "You know," I said, "I could use your help. Rainbow hasn't had his exercise yet today. Would you like to take him for a walk?"

The girl glanced down at her wheels. "Me?"

"Absolutely you. Rainbow would love to walk down the halls with you."

The room filled with excitement as a nurse got everything ready and pushed the girl through the doorway in her wheelchair. Jorge extended a blue webbed lead, which had a

58

double line so that she could hold one end while Jorge held the other end for safety.

"Ready?" he asked, standing back so the girl would think she was doing it all by herself. Rainbow's tiny hooves clicked against the shiny floor as he matched his pace with the movement of the wheelchair. Holding the lead, the girl sat up taller in her chair. She proudly waved to nurses and doctors and beamed as everyone watched them pass by. As they made a triumphant loop of the entire floor, the smile never left her face. Afterward, the nurse helped her into bed, and we let her choose her own stuffed horse to remember our time together. "I just knew I'd get to walk a horse today!" she said as we left.

In the next room, a young boy was lying in bed, connected to IVs, oxygen, and monitors. His parents sat close by, their hands folded in prayer. Rainbow walked up to the bedside and leaned in close. The boy had been asleep but roused when he sensed the warm breath tickling his shoulders. As he opened his eyes, life seemed to come into him. He leaned close and put his cheek against the horse's smooth nose. Rainbow nuzzled him softly. They stayed together that way for many minutes.

While the boy gazed intently at the horse, the parents focused on their son, and I watched the parents. We were there for the family members too—for the moms, dads, and siblings every bit as much as the patient. The boy's parents had been through a lot with their son's cancer diagnosis. Now I saw their furrowed brows soften. Their eyes welled up, and for a time they were lifted away from a place of worry and exhaustion. Perhaps they had never imagined their child could feel happy given these circumstances. But there he was smiling, and hope settled around them. Rainbow had been able to provide a break from their troubled thoughts, and such a break can be powerful. When we are able to pull away from something difficult for a while, that's when we're open to finding something to grasp hold of—something to encourage us that no matter what, we're going to get through it okay. Rainbow helped that family experience hope—I felt it settling in the room as we left for our next stop.

The staff member led us to a few more rooms. At the end of the hall near a nursing station full of monitors, we approached a door that was slightly ajar. "We can just bypass this room," the aide said in a hushed voice. I nodded, and we had started to move on when a woman rushed out and called after us, "Wait! You're not going to come in?" She ran a hand over her rumpled outfit—she'd obviously been sleeping in her clothes. Her face was drawn, with dark circles under her eyes. I recognized the expression—the look of a worried parent.

I turned and checked with the staff member, who nodded and smiled. "Of course we'll come in," I said.

We led Rainbow back and into the room. As we entered, I saw why the guide had suggested we move on. A small boy lay completely still in the bed. He had a tracheotomy to help him breathe, and he appeared to be asleep, possibly sedated or in a coma. We never ask. His mom had clearly been sitting with him day after day, night after night. She leaned over the bed rail. Although there was no way to know if he could hear her, she spoke lovingly to her child. "There's a pony in the room." She touched his cheek. He didn't stir.

Jorge and Rainbow moved to the edge of the bed. The mom kissed her son's little hand. Then she gently pulled his hand over and placed it on the horse's nose. She moved it in a patting motion and smiled softly. Jorge stepped back and let her have the moment with her son. The boy may not have known we were there, but it mattered to the mom. It mattered.

After visiting a few more rooms, we left the pediatric ward and took the elevator back down to the lobby. At the heavy front doors, I took a moment to reflect. Our visits were happy times, and I always kept my focus on that positivity and the good we could do for others. Yet sometimes a bit of the sadness of an ill child or a worried parent stuck with me as I thought of all they were going through. And I knew that no matter how many young patients we visited and saw through to recovery, there would always be more ill children in need of comfort and love. A comfort that, as a volunteer, I sometimes needed myself and also received from the horses. The horses got me through and gave me encouragement. They helped me when I was down, tired, or hurting. That was how I could keep going back to the places where people needed love and hope, even if doing so was at times difficult. And almost always, even in the most upsetting experiences, I took away something sweet and profound.

One time we stopped in the oncology ward to see Alex, a boy who had spent long months in the hospital as he battled cancer. During that time Magic had been to see him probably a dozen times. On this particular visit, Magic lingered as Alex held her face with special tenderness, rubbing his hand along her jaw, cheek, and forehead. It seemed as if their two souls were touching. "I want to remember what she looks like," he said. A nurse later informed me that complications of his disease were causing Alex to lose his sight. Magic meant so much to his recovery that he was trying to etch each detail of her face into his mind.

Another time we were asked to grant the wish of a little girl at home in hospice care. She had asked to have a tea party with the horses. It was a wonderful, creative request, and Jorge and I were honored to help make it come true. We brought four horses to her home, each one dressed in bedazzled outfits. The horses never mind wearing a costume for a short time, and we are always careful that the costumes are safe and comfortable. Several of our volunteers joined us so that each horse had its own handler, with others forming a little perimeter around us to answer any questions and make sure all the interactions went smoothly.

When we arrived, the little girl was waiting for us. She wore a pink tutu and a sun hat with satin ribbons and bows. Colorful balloons decorated the room, and a child-sized table was set with picnic food and a pink frosted cake. The little girl's friends were there wearing party hats and fancy dress-up clothes. Jorge and the volunteers led the horses right up to the picnic table, and everyone gathered around, smiling and laughing. I was moved to see them sharing a happy moment, creating a memory for the family. The tea party couldn't have been any more magical.

One of my most cherished visits was the time we stopped in the room of a sweet preschooler who had been refusing to eat. Chemotherapy had taken away the girl's appetite and caused painful sores in her mouth. She squealed with delight, however, when Magic came into her room. It did everyone good to see the child so happy. We were about to leave when the girl's dinner tray arrived. "Why don't we stay a little bit longer?" Jorge suggested. Magic tossed her head, as if agreeing. To everyone's surprise, with the girl's attention focused on the horse, she gobbled up her entire meal. Afterward, everyone laughed as she mischievously balanced the bowl on her head like any toddler might do. Magic even stayed a little longer while I read the sleepy child a bedtime story, and when we left, our hearts were lighter.

Only later, when we were at the front doors and getting ready to leave the hospital, did my mind go to a very sad and difficult place. The little girl was so sweet; she tugged at my maternal side. But I'd never had a chance to feed a baby of my own. To sit on the edge of a bed and read my child a story. To watch my own sweet infant grow up and take those first steps, ride a bike, go to school, get married. I'd never know the joy of holding grandchildren on my knee.

You see, God didn't give me and Jorge biological children, the family I had dreamed of since I was a young girl. I cultivated my nurturing side by babysitting, developing a passion for teaching by playing school with my young charges and helping them learn and write the alphabet. When I got my first job as a real teacher, I poured all my energy, creativity, and loving care into those students. It felt good that they cared about me too. After Jorge and I got married, we decided to adopt older children. Adoption can be a wonderful blessing, but we had a different and challenging experience. Life isn't all neat and tidy—it doesn't always hand you what you want. So that day, as Jorge, Rainbow, and I walked out of the hospital after reading to that sweet toddler, those painful feelings cropped up and tumbled around inside me.

We crossed the parking lot and found a stretch of grass. Just as I sometimes feel a heaviness after seeing what these children and their families go through, I believe that the horses can feel the weight of these visits too. They clearly sense that they are there for a purpose and can pick up on moods in the room. That is one reason individual horses work no more than two visits a week. Jorge and I also limit the length of time they work to avoid tiring them out and overloading them with emotion, and we also give them a cooling-off time after every visit.

"Shake it off," Jorge told Rainbow as he let out the slack in the long lead line. Rainbow ran and kicked his legs and shook his mane. His long tail flowed behind him. There was no way to watch him without feeling the joy of every graceful movement. And in that moment I felt the weight lessen, and I was able to shake it off too.

Maybe what I'd gone through was for a reason. I thought of the parents, the ones I had just watched at their child's bedside. Those parents were going through something difficult. It wasn't the same as my experience, but sad is sad. Hard is hard. It's not a contest. We all face worries and doubts. Some parents have to face losing their beloved child. Maybe, just maybe, my experience was meant to grow my empathy so I could help someone else. Maybe that was one reason why I was drawn to bring our horses to the intensive care units, the trauma wards, and the very bleakest, scariest places. It wasn't the same, but I'd been there too.

There will always be hardships. But there is always hope. I cling to that. That is the only way I know how to shake it off.

6

"We see little miracles all the time."

PawPaw had been in hospice care for some time, and it became clear to his family that the end was nearing. As his loved ones gathered at his bedside, they heard him uttering one word: "Faith."

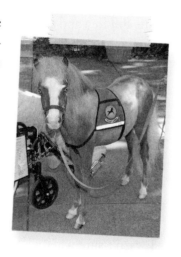

His wife called us and asked if we could bring one of our horses to visit. She explained that her husband was not calling out for spiritual strength. "Faith was his childhood pony." Now, in his final days, his mind had drifted back to happier times. I imagined him remembering himself in a wonderful place with tall grass and dandelions, the smell of fresh hay, and the

67

warmth of the sun on his shoulders, running together with his barnyard friend across endless stretches of green field.

When we arrived at PawPaw's house, a hospice worker met us outside. "I don't know if you still want to go in," she said. "I'm afraid he slipped into a coma this morning." She glanced at Magic and shook her head. "He might not even know you're here."

Jorge just smiled. We never assumed what a patient could or couldn't hear. In our experience, the horses helped exactly who they were meant to help, whatever the circumstances. We were still willing to bring Magic inside. No matter what, we'd be there for the family.

Magic tapped along beside us to PawPaw's bedroom. He was lying motionless on his back, eyes closed, a crisp coverlet pulled up to his chin, one arm resting outside the blanket. His children and grandchildren filled the room and encircled the bed—they all looked up and stepped aside for Magic when we entered.

Magic eased up to the bedside. We always felt as if she had a special sense for situations like this and let her do what came naturally. She studied the gentleman, standing there for a moment or two, gently tossing her shiny black mane. Then she softly lowered her head and laid it on PawPaw's arm. Jorge and I stood back and waited. There wasn't a sound in the room. The children and grandchildren barely budged. Magic gazed at the man. Then the covers rustled. At first I wasn't sure whether Magic was causing the movement or not—but no, Magic remained absolutely still. Very slowly the man's hand started moving, working its way up to Magic's face. A weathered forefinger extended and rubbed against the side of her nose. Magic softly nuzzled back. PawPaw's eyes fluttered open for a moment. He laid his hand gently on Magic's head while his family watched through their tears. Then his eyes closed and his arm fell.

Magic served a dual purpose that day, easing the beloved patriarch out of his coma for one last precious moment, then comforting the children and young grandchildren as they gathered around her for tender hugs and pats.

"I can barely believe it," the hospice worker told us later.

"We see little miracles all the time," Jorge answered.

This is true. We've seen seemingly unresponsive patients react. We've seen those who are nonverbal find a special way to communicate. Some of the most endearing moments happen when a person has a history of horses in their life. Sometimes a horse, even a miniature one, is a catalyst for memories. The sound of tiny hooves clopping down the hospital hall often brings to mind the sound of hoofbeats pounding across scenic trails. The smell of a leather halter brings back days of working in a barn. I often hear stories of a horse from the past when we spend time with older adults.

One cool afternoon we brought Magic to a quiet sitting area in an assisted living home. We were there to visit Earl, a thin, dignified man who leaned forward in his chair, eager to greet us. It was clear he was familiar with horses. Not only did he appear completely at ease when Magic approached, but he knew just where to place his hands and how to talk to her. Magic walked right up to him and rested her head on his lap. I could almost picture the little horse smiling as she let out a contented sigh. Their instant connection felt so right.

Earl didn't talk much when we met him, but he held an album full of old photos. Together we leafed through the pages and admired photos of a young man on horseback. A nurse leaned over and said, "Did you know that you're talking to a star here? Earl used to be in the movies."

"He was? Which ones? Would I have seen them?" I asked.

"Earl was a stunt double in the old-time Westerns. You know, like with Roy Rogers and the Lone Ranger."

"A stunt double," I said. "Oh Earl, that is amazing! I've seen many of those old Western movies. Maybe I was really watching you and never even knew it!"

Earl nodded and seemed to drift off to a time long ago, when he was not an older man in a nursing home but a rugged cowboy in the saddle. He lowered his face close to Magic's. I knew how sad I would feel being around horses my entire life and then having to be separated from these creatures I held so dear. It was my privilege to be able to bring a horse into Earl's life again. Earl was so happy to be around a horse, in fact, that he followed us up and down the halls for the rest of the visit. We couldn't bear to leave until after he had sat back down and fallen asleep.

I often think about people like Earl and the lives they have lived—those who love horses but no longer have the opportunity to be around them. Once we went to the home of a very ill older woman who had been an equestrian all her life. As we walked into her living room, we passed shelves and tables full of framed horse photos. She spent the whole afternoon hugging our horse and recounting happy stories of her past. Having a horse visit her in her own home connected that woman not only to memories but to her life's passion, her own personal value and significance.

One woman we met loved watching old Western movies. Every day she would lie in bed and watch her Westerns on the television, so Jorge and I planned a surprise for her. We dressed Cloudburst and Mozart in cowboy costumes—brown fringed vests and red bandanas, complete with black cowboy hats perched atop their heads. We walked the horses into the building and down the hall. When we peeked into this woman's room, there she was lying in bed, and sure enough, an old black-and-white Western flickered on the TV.

Jorge straightened the little cowboy hats. "She's going to love you two," I said, clicking on my iPod. An old cowboy song started playing: "Happy trails to you . . ."

On cue, our horses carefully walked into the room. They stepped right in front of the TV as a scene of horses running across a field played on the screen. The woman sat straight up, her eyes wide, and her jaw dropped. She couldn't move for several minutes; she was so surprised. Then she laughed with delight. We brought Cloudburst to her bedside, and she hugged the horse with all her might. She must have thought it was a miracle to have real horses in her room.

Another woman in an assisted living facility had been just as delighted to meet the horses. Her daughter even called us one day to say that her mother told her there had been a horse in her room. The daughter said, "I was concerned. I called her caretakers right away and asked if they thought Mom had taken a turn for the worse. I told them, 'She thinks there was a horse in the room.' They laughed and told me there really had been a horse in her room!" We got a good chuckle out of her story.

One afternoon when we walked into the lobby of a care facility, a woman was sitting right in front of the doors waiting for us, an antique picture frame in her lap. "I heard you were coming today," she said. "I didn't want to miss you!"

A staff member rushed over to join us. "She's been sitting in this spot all morning, wouldn't move an inch." Then she lowered her voice and told me, "We're so pleased! She hasn't been out of her room in six months."

Magic shuffled her feet, delighted to meet this new friend. The woman showed Magic the frame with a black-and-white photo of herself as a young girl with a big bow in her hair and riding a pony. "Look!" she said. I let the two have their little chat. Magic's visit had stirred memories of the woman's childhood horse and awakened her desire to get out and reconnect with the world. She'd even found the courage to leave her room after many months, just to be sure she wouldn't miss seeing a miniature horse who brought her such happiness.

Magic also found a special friend in the memory care facility, a curly-haired woman who always dashed as fast as her legs would take her to greet Magic. One time as we approached, she scurried out to meet us. "You're back!" she said, her voice singsong with delight. Her son, who was visiting that day, followed behind. The woman lowered herself to her knees and hugged the horse. "Hiya, Magic. Hiya, my old friend."

The son took in the scene and shook his head. "How can this be?" he asked. "How can this be? She doesn't even know who *I* am!"

Several weeks later, as I was making preparations to bring three horses to a new facility, a staff member called and said,

"Thank you for arranging this, but I just wanted to let you know that I won't be there on the day you visit."

"Oh, I'm sorry," I said. "Would you like us to reschedule?" There was a long pause on the other end. "You see . . ." Another long pause. "Years ago I was in a serious riding accident. And now . . . now I can't even drive by a pasture without feeling panicky, much less be in the same room as a horse. I'm sorry, I won't be there to meet you."

"I understand," I said. "But just so you know, our horses are very small and calm. I think you'd be okay with them, if you change your mind."

"I'll think about it," the woman said.

The day Jorge and I and several volunteers walked the horses into the facility, the woman who had made the arrangements was nowhere around. "That's too bad," I said. Her feelings were certainly understandable, yet I always regretted when people had a negative reaction to horses. Meeting a friendly, gentle miniature horse might have been one step in helping the woman get over her fears.

We were led to a sunny community room where we met Hilda, sitting in her wheelchair. Magic perked right up. I can tell when Magic is extra interested in a person, and the little horse was definitely interested in Hilda. Hilda was quiet and reserved, yet looked surprised to see a horse inside. I saw a sparkle in her eyes, bright and alert, taking in everything. Magic walked right up to the chair and put her head in Hilda's lap. As she touched the horse's mane, Hilda seemed to come awake, like a flower opening in the sunlight. Hilda looked Magic in the eyes. Then she clearly said, "Isn't she beautiful!"

The reaction in the room was immediate . . . and puzzling. The staff who were present gasped, and one of them began

73

to cry. Someone ran out and brought back several others, and they all stood there smiling and wiping away tears. One of them returned with a woman who held a clipboard and hesitated before entering.

"It's a horse!" Hilda said, and everyone started crying again.

I looked around, confused. "What's going on?" I whispered.

"Hilda . . . she hasn't spoken since I arrived here," a young man said. "Not one word in three years."

Now Jorge and I fully understood the significance of the powerful connection. The woman with the clipboard then walked over and hugged Hilda. "I want you to know, I love you," she said.

Hilda looked up, smiling. "I love you too."

Magic ignored all the excitement and focused on Hilda, nuzzling her softly and looking her in the eyes. As we left, Hilda called after us, "Will you come back again?"

"For sure, Hilda," Jorge said. "Just for you."

As we left, someone tapped me on the shoulder. It was the woman with the clipboard. "I'm the one you spoke to on the phone. I can't believe what just happened. It's a miracle. As you know, I wasn't going to come in today, but something told me to. Somehow I gathered up the courage. Now I know why."

Jorge smiled. That day we saw a double miracle—Hilda talking, and the staff member taking a step toward healing from her fears.

Another person who took healing steps—literally—is a man named Pastor John. John is a (now retired) minister who had been in an accident and was recovering at a rehabilitation center, where he took a liking to Wakanda. When we first met John, he couldn't sit up, yet he always remained positive. "I'm going to get better," he said. "You'll see."

We visited him many times, sometimes in the beautiful garden area outside the rehab building. On one of our visits, he was learning how to get around with an electric wheelchair. "I won't need this for long," he said. "I'm going to walk again."

"Would you like Wakanda to walk with you?" Jorge asked. The horses often spend time working with people in rehab to help improve their motor skills. Patients exercise their legs by walking with the horses and strengthen their arms by brushing them. John agreed. The physical therapist told us what was needed, and Wakanda moved her slender, stockinged leg a slow step forward. John accelerated his wheelchair.

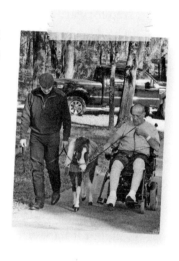

Then Wakanda moved again. John maneuvered the chair. They made it down the length of the path, made a wide turn, and returned. "Don't get used to this, little gal," John said with a smile. "I'm going to walk again."

Before John was discharged, he'd made great progress with his mobility. He truly believed that he'd walk again, no matter what anyone else said. Even when things were difficult, he had faith. As he stood next to Wakanda, I'll never forget what he said to her: "One day I'll come back and walk to you."

About a year after John was discharged, we heard that he'd returned to the area and wanted to see us. Jorge and I brought Wakanda as quickly as we could. When we approached the rehab building, John was there in the garden, sitting in a chair alongside the path. His wife stood by his side. They both smiled, happy to see us. Wakanda tossed her head, eager to greet him. "Wait," he said. We stopped.

He gripped the arms of his chair and pulled himself up. "This is for you, Wakanda." He let go of the chair and took a step forward.

I held my breath. John took another step toward Wakanda. His wife followed closely with a walker at the ready. With each step, John's smile grew. After several steps, Wakanda pranced forward to meet him. He stopped to catch his breath and reached out for her.

"Hooray!" Jorge and I cheered and clapped for him.

"We did it!" John said, hugging Wakanda. He never gave up. I was impressed by his faith and courage.

I never grow tired of witnessing the way the horses help people heal and find strength. Sometimes it's difficult to explain, but it happens over and over.

Through the years, we've been invited to attend a number of events for Gold Star families—the immediate relatives of US Armed Forces members who have died in combat. I always accept invitations to bring the horses to these events because of my experience with my father being away in the service, and I remember how difficult that was on my mother, my brothers, and me. "In military families, the children serve too. They have to spend time without a parent," I told Jorge. Whenever we are at such an event, I always keep alert for the parent, the spouse, and especially the child who seems to need extra attention.

At one Gold Star event we attended at a school cafeteria, I noticed a girl sitting all alone in a corner with her head down. I learned that she had recently lost her father. After the ceremony, I approached the girl. "Would you like to take Magic for a walk?" I asked. She nodded.

Jorge and I led the girl and Magic outside. Jorge handed her the lead and took the other end of the double line. I walked along beside her. The girl remained quiet for a while. When she finally started talking, she opened up to Magic about her father. "He took me to the movies," she said.

They made another circle around the grassy path. "We ate ice cream together."

Slowly, they walked down a hill. "He got me some Barbie dolls for Christmas."

They turned the corner. The girl bent down and ran her hands over Magic's neck. She put her face close and barely whispered, "He said he would come back."

I swallowed hard. "He would have if he could," I said. The girl looked up, her eyes wide, and nodded. Then she kept walking. After several more trips around, it was time to go. She hugged Magic and the healing began. A little miracle that is just as amazing as first words or first steps.

Miracles conveyed in a glance or a touch—they are possible any time the horses come together with people who are hurting. The restorative healing of a mini horse and mighty hope.

7

"I was there."

Happy anniversary," I said, squinting as the unfamiliar room came into focus. It felt strange to be lying there in the luxurious bed, surrounded by a peaceful quietness, the smell of crisp white linens, and a bathroom full of fancy soaps. I had to pinch myself to remember that we were in Seattle, more than three thousand miles from Florida, the farm, and the horses.

Jorge and I had celebrated our twenty-third anniversary the day before, on December 14, 2012, and that weekend was the first time we'd gotten away in a long time. It was time to focus on each other. With the early morning sun streaming through the window, I allowed the relaxation to wash over me. I was ready for a day together exploring the town and seeing the sights.

My cell phone rang.

"Who could be calling?" Jorge asked.

"Maybe there's something wrong back home?" Although a dependable caretaker was looking after the horses and had a private number to call for emergencies, I couldn't help worrying. My brows knit as I listened to the caller. "Yes, we heard. I'm so sorry. How terrible. I understand. Of course, we'll see what we can do."

I turned to Jorge. "That was a secretary from the town hall in Newtown, Connecticut."

Jorge's eyes widened. "The town in the news? The shooting yesterday?"

We'd both seen live reports of the shocking events at Sandy Hook Elementary School. Images of terrified students rushing out of the school single file, their hands on the shoulders of the person ahead of them. Images of anxious parents clinging to crying children. The shooting left twenty of those elementary students and six heroic adult staff members dead. I had barely been able to believe my eyes when I watched the coverage. And now someone from Newtown was reaching out to us.

"She follows us on Facebook. She said the community wants us to come."

"Us?" It was more of a statement of wonder than a question. Could we really do this? We sat silently, each considering the obstacles. It would be a long trip. The horses weren't adapted to the cold weather up north. Such a venture was expensive and would require more funds than we had in our budget. And what about our vacation, our anniversary?

80

Yet the words "Sandy Hook" loomed larger than any of the questions. As an educator, the horror of the school shooting hit me hard. What would I have done if it had happened to my students, in my classroom, in my school? How would I be able to bear the loss of lives? If there was one small thing, anything, I could do to help people through the painful aftermath of this tragedy, I would do it.

Instead of painting the town, we spent our anniversary making plans in our hotel room.

When we finally walked downstairs for dinner, we were still sorting out details. As we waited for our table, Jorge called some of our devoted volunteers. "They've asked us to come to Newtown, Connecticut," he said. "Can you get away?" He explained the situation over and over, describing what we'd need to pull it off. "The horses aren't used to the winter weather. We'll have to gather heavy blankets. We'll need an indoor riding ring so the horses can exercise. Extra helpers in Newtown. Do you know where we might find a heated trailer?"

We barely tasted our entrées as we hunched over our lists and calendars. When the waiter came to clear the dishes, he didn't bring us a bill. "Your dinner tonight is taken care of," he said with a slight bow. "A gentleman overheard you speaking in the lobby about what you're going to do and wanted to thank you." Jorge and I looked around to see who might have done the good deed, but the benefactor must have wished to remain anonymous. We hadn't even left for Connecticut yet, and already we were overwhelmed with a generous gift of support. It never occurred to us that someone would extend such a kindness, and it humbled us.

We abandoned our anniversary vacation and flew back to Florida that night.

During the flight we wrote page after page of lists. At home we made numerous phone calls to coordinate countless arrangements. Despite my organized nature, the logistics were daunting. We arranged for six volunteers to join us in Connecticut.

"How are you going to pull this off?" a friend asked. "Where will the horses stay? How will you get there? How will you find out who needs help?"

"There are some calls you just can't say no to," I answered. "We said yes first, and now we'll make it happen."

Amazingly, generosity continued our way—help arrived. Because our trailer wasn't heated, a professional horse transport service offered their powerful trucks and trailers, state-of-the-art equipment, and heated stalls. An airline donated plane tickets. A hotel donated lodging. One woman sewed beautiful, warm blankets for the horses out of blue-and-gold brocade. An equine emergency transport company volunteered to shuttle the miniatures to events around town. An equestrian center in Newtown graciously offered us the use of their barns and indoor ring. It was all the more poignant because one of the girls lost in the shooting had been learning to ride there.

After a week of making arrangements, Jorge and I walked Magic, Aladdin, and Wakanda into the sleek trailer. These horses all had experience in a school setting and were calm and dependable. I took a deep breath as I stood in our

82

driveway, watching the truck and trailer pull away. This was the only time any of the horses had gone anywhere without us. I felt like a mother watching her children go off to school. Fortunately, Jorge and I took a flight so that we would be there to greet the horses in Connecticut when they arrived.

When our plane landed in New York City, we headed over to the nearest car rental counter. Although many people were helping, we still needed to manage our budget.

"We'd like to rent a van. We've traveled up from Florida to volunteer at Sandy Hook Elementary School. Is there any way you'd be able to offer us a discount?" Jorge asked.

The woman behind the counter frowned and shuffled some papers. She looked skeptical. "How is it you're volunteering, again?"

Over the background din of a television, Jorge explained what we were there to do. The woman shook her head. "I'd like to help, but what is it you're doing, again?"

A man's voice boomed behind us. "This is the home of Gentle Carousel in central Florida."

Jorge and I turned to see a reporter from CNN on the airport lobby television. A prerecorded video clip of our farm played on the TV screen. "These hero horses are on their way to Newtown, Connecticut, to bring comfort to those affected by the tragic shootings," the reporter announced.

We stood frozen, staring at the television. I pointed and said, "That's us! This is what we've come to do!"

The rental company donated their services.

After securing the van, Jorge drove us and the volunteers to Newtown. The idyllic little town with white steeples and distant snowy hills seemed discordant with the horrors that had recently shattered the lives of the people there. A festive wreathed lamppost stood unconvincingly beside a flagpole with its flag at half-staff.

When we pulled up to the farm, the owners and workers came out to meet us. They showed us around and graciously offered us anything we needed. Despite so much sadness, we were greeted so warmly.

That night we all went to the hotel except Jorge, who stayed behind to huddle in the heated horse van where he would spend the night with Magic, Aladdin, and Wakanda. Although the equestrian center had beautiful barns and stalls, they weren't heated. With the single-digit temperatures and our Florida horses' shorter coats, we did everything possible to ensure they stayed warm, comfortable, and well-supervised. We'd each take a turn spending the night with them in the van.

For the first few days, the horses visited privately with grief-stricken families. Then the staff of Newtown's Booth Library arranged a group event for that Saturday. Although they'd sent out an email notice, they were unsure what the response would be. "I don't know how many will show up," one of the organizers told me. "We may get only two or three."

"Then we'll be here for those two or three," I said.

We set up in a meeting room. Magic wore a beautiful gold-embroidered blanket. The other horses waited with a volunteer in the heated trailer in the parking lot.

When the doors opened, there were six hundred people lined up!

The librarian organized the waiting families into smaller groups. We made room on the carpeted floor. I opened a book and began to read. After the story, Jorge returned

Magic to the volunteer in the heated trailer and brought out Aladdin, and then later Wakanda, so that each horse would get a chance to participate and a chance to rest. Each child took a turn patting and hugging the horses. I hoped they would find the courage they needed to heal and move on.

The next morning I opened a copy of *USA Today*, which had been slid under our hotel room door. There was Magic's picture! In the accompanying article, a librarian described the excitement of the horses and all the young people in the library. She explained that it was a step forward in healing, a step toward getting back to normal for the community. It felt good to know how our visit had helped and how the librarian felt. I hoped that day marked the beginning of her healing too.

Later in the week, we gathered in a huge gymnasium. A line wrapped all the way around the gym. In such a small town, everyone had a friend, relative, sibling, or neighbor who had been involved in the shooting. My heart ached—the need for solace was so great. As each child took a turn, some told the horses what they'd seen and how they were feeling. Jorge and I and the other volunteers just listened and let the horses do the work.

From time to time, I looked up and noticed a man wearing a dark blue windbreaker, hunched in a folding chair. He held his baseball cap in his hands and sat so still he barely seemed to take a breath. He watched as the children patted and hugged the horses. When I had a moment, I approached. The logo on his jacket was that of a nearby fire department. "Would you like to come over?" I asked.

He blinked as if coming out of a trance and shook his head. "Oh no, it's for the kids," he said. "I'm just watching."

I smiled and walked back. After a while we changed horses so they could take a break. When I looked, the man was still there. Hours later, as the line began to dwindle, I approached the solemn man again. "Everyone is almost gone. Do you want to come over now?"

"I don't know," he said.

"We're not just here for the children." I motioned for him to follow. "We're here for everyone."

He rose slowly. I led him over to where Magic was standing. He patted her, his expression remaining stoic. He was so broken, I wondered if we could do enough to help. Then he sat down on the floor and looked directly into Magic's eyes. There was a long pause, a deep breath, another pause. At last he spoke.

"I was there," he whispered.

After that, the words tumbled out. "I was at the gas station when I was called." His hands fumbled. "Now I can't pass that gas station without a wrench in my gut." I waited for him to go on, but he couldn't talk about the terrible things he saw. He just said, "No one should have to see that." He put his arms around Magic and held her for a long time. At last he wiped his eyes and pulled his windbreaker tighter around him. When he stood up, the stoic expression was back. He took Jorge's hand, then mine. "Thank you," he said, and very quietly walked out the door.

After four and a half hours, we took the horses outside to shake it off and returned them to the indoor arena where they could exercise. As I watched them run and play, I thought of the children who would no longer have that opportunity. *Shake it off*, I reminded myself. *Shake it off.*

The one-week stay extended to two. "It's so sad," I said one night in our hotel room. "Everyone is in pain."

"And yet there's so much compassion." Jorge put his arm around me. "Notice the way people are treating each other? Holding doors, looking out for each other, going out of their way. The ribbons and the banners of support in the stores and windows."

"And the way they're responding to us," I said. "Remember that old man who drove all over town searching for us, just to bring us a thermos of hot chocolate? And yesterday, the little girl who came up and gave us her allowance money for the horses." So much unity and benevolence had come out of the tragedy. The wounds cut deep, yet the love was strong. We went to sleep, exhausted but grateful.

The next morning we visited the preschool directly across the street from the elementary school. Many of the Sandy Hook children had attended there when they were younger. About two dozen three- and four-year-old children sat crosslegged on the carpet. I smiled and held a handmade book in my lap. "I'm going to read you a story," I said.

A small girl in the front row slowly raised her hand. "Does anyone die in this story?"

Her words tugged at my heart. "Oh no," I said softly. "This is a story about a very special horse and all her friends." I shared the book, which contained a moral about loving and respecting each other.

87

After the story, each child took a turn hugging Magic, feeling her warmth and love. Magic looked right into their eyes and responded to their embraces. Troubled faces gave way to joyful expressions, and tightly pressed lips turned into smiles. The atmosphere in the room was transformed. After everyone had their turn and Jorge and I prepared to leave, one of the children started to sing.

I later learned that the children in school had always loved to sing. The song was not a typical preschool ditty but a catchy tune they'd learned in class. They loved it because of the bouncy tune and the fun call-and-response element. The song was called "Build Me Up Buttercup."

"Why don't you build me up," the child began.

The other preschoolers echoed, "Build me up . . ."

"Buttercup," the first child sang.

More children joined in the echo. "Buttercup . . ."

Their sweet, innocent voices rang out. One teacher put her hand to her mouth while another blinked back tears. Later, they told me that it was the first time the children had sung since the tragedy. The more the children sang, the more I felt their heavy hearts lighten bit by bit. Their voices grew louder as Jorge, Magic, and I walked out the door, waving. Nothing touched me quite so deeply as that preschool visit. Those children were strong, and I hoped and prayed they would heal.

We tried to consider every possible group of people who might benefit from a visit—students, parents, teachers. Our last stop was at the Newtown police station. Jorge and I recognize that first responders to a tragedy are also affected by the experience.

The men and women took turns in the tiny interrogation room where we sat with Magic. Some stroked Magic's neck, others hugged her tight. Each officer had a chance for a few private moments. The emotion in the room ran deep.

The police officers joined us to walk Magic back outside. Along the way, we stopped in different offices down the hall to say goodbye. When we got to one closed door, an officer shook his head. "Too bad Chief isn't here today. He'd like to see this."

"We could take a picture," another suggested.

"Yes, a picture," the others agreed. "Let's do it." They led us into the office, where we posed Magic next to the chief's chair. Magic nosed the paperwork scattered atop the desk. As the officers in the room snapped pictures on their cell phones, I felt something unexpected fill that room—the tension started to break and the sadness lifted just a little. A staff member turned to me and said, "This is the first time I've seen them smile since it happened." I was glad that Magic had given the dedicated police officers a chance to smile and not feel guilty. It didn't mean that they hurt any less. It was just a momentary break from the difficult, emotionally taxing work.

Before leaving Connecticut, we stopped to pay our respects at the memorials that had sprung up around town. I rubbed my hands together to keep them warm. A snow-covered pile of bouquets, framed photographs, toys, and stuffed animals grew outside the town hall. On one side stood a Christmas tree decorated with angels. Simple, hand-lettered signs declared,

We're with you in spirit.

You're in our prayers.

Be strong.

People with nothing else in common came together, clung to each other, and supported each other. A mother had lost her child. A boy had lost his friend. They came from all over to stand there and remember. Draped in their warm blankets, the horses stood reverently among the crowd. One teen girl stopped to hug Magic after placing a small teddy bear with a Santa hat on the pile. She and her family had come from out of state to pay their respects. "I just needed to be here," she said, unable to explain her emotions.

We stayed for as long as we could, but it was time to go home. As we turned to walk back to the van, gentle flurries began. The horses' first snowfall. They looked up, tilting their heads curiously. Lacy flakes settled on their noses.

As I walked beside them, my mind crowded with thoughts of all these miniature horses had done, of the encouragement they had provided. The type of support that was essential for the grieving people of Newtown, to give them confidence that there really is good in the world. To give them hope that, despite the circumstances, better times would come again.

I looked at the horses amid the fresh, invigorating snow. Magic trotted. Aladdin leapt. Wakanda swished her long tail, prancing in the falling flakes. It felt like joy. It felt a little bit like healing.

8

"They can tolerate things, but they shouldn't have to."

Scout jumped up and placed his feet atop his mother's back, trying to get a better vantage point. The mare stood patiently. I often thought that Wakanda must be the most tolerant mom around. And Scout, the friskiest foal.

Scout was born on a muggy night in July, when even the setting sun gave no relief from the heat. The fans in the stalls whirred, keeping the horses comfortable. That night Wakanda's halter, which sent a signal whenever she would lie flat, sounded the alarm. Jorge and I checked the

video monitors that allow us to see everything that is happening in the barn and ran out to observe the birth. The delivery was swift, easy, and beautiful, and shortly afterward Scout looked me right in the eyes, as if to say hello. He was tiny—just over five pounds—but for one so small, he had enormous energy. He popped up within minutes and soon was taking his first shaky steps, figuring out how to walk and how to run and leaping through the air. *Look, I'm doing it!* he seemed to say. He marched right over to us to say hello. Jorge and I checked him all over, getting him used to being touched. Then he began nursing and settling in with his mother.

"He's a bold little guy," Jorge said. Scout didn't seem afraid of anything. We were able to be hands-on with Scout because Wakanda trusted us and because Jorge and I were respectful of her. Even at this tender age, we began preparing Scout for his training to be a therapy horse. Each of our horses goes through a two-year basic training period. All Scout's early training would be done alongside his mother.

Every morning starts with a quick assessment of all the horses and then the first feeding. Jorge loads hay, powdered minerals, and forage onto the back of our off-road utility vehicle and delivers it across the acreage. Horses in the wild graze all day, and Jorge and I spread out the food so the little herd can move from food source to food source.

As the other horses scattered out into the large pasture, Scout and Wakanda stayed in their separate penned area, where the other horses could still stop by and safely say hello. We are never in a hurry to wean our foals. Baby Scout loved to circle the big outdoor enclosure, bounding on long, gangly legs and kicking up tufts of grass while Wakanda grazed peacefully close by. He ran rings around his mother, then suddenly wheeled around and galloped off in the other direction. I imagined Wakanda felt relieved her little one wasn't jumping up on her or pestering her during those moments. There were so few opportunities of relief from this frisky foal!

Scout grew stronger and bolder. When he was ready, we led him around the farm, practicing walking on different surfaces. Sometimes we placed different objects in the pen—a stool, mounting steps, a wheelchair. Scout nosed them and poked them as he learned to accept changes in his environment. Of course, like any youngster, Scout mostly enjoyed playtime.

"He really likes that Jolly Ball," I said one afternoon. Scout kicked the soft plastic toy across the grass. "He's enthusiastic, that's for sure."

"Maybe a little too much." Jorge chuckled, stepping aside as the little one came charging his way. Scout enjoyed playing with another young horse, Anthem, and he particularly enjoyed Anthem's favorite toy, a large, soft rubber ball with a black-and-white soccer design that we affectionately referred to as Wilson. Anthem slept with Wilson at night, secure with it next to him much like a child with their favorite blanket. If Anthem went anywhere in the trailer, Wilson also had to ride along. The two were inseparable.

"Look, Scout got Wilson again," Jorge said. Sure enough, Scout ran past, kicking the soccer ball through the grass. While Anthem was gentle with his precious Wilson, Scout was rambunctious and careless. Anthem carefully pushed Wilson along. Scout kicked it hard. Whenever Scout got hold of Wilson, Anthem trotted anxiously behind.

"I'd better help." Jorge set out to intervene. But Scout decided that the best way to play that day was to take a nice roll on top of Wilson, over and over again.

Pop!

Anthem stopped short at the sudden bang.

"Oh no, Scout broke Wilson!" Jorge said. He tried to retrieve it, but Scout trotted off, merrily tossing around the deflated ball.

"I'm so sorry, Anthem." I crouched beside the gentle white horse. "We'll fix it. We'll try, I promise."

It turned out that when people read Gentle Carousel's Facebook post about Anthem's misfortune, they were moved to help, and the miniature horse ended up with a half dozen new, unpopped Wilsons to love.

With the foals, every experience is an opportunity for training. While out walking them on a halter, I might drop my keys or have someone clang a bell in the distance to get them used to sudden noises. Scout learned to stand still for brushing and having his hooves trimmed. With Wakanda nearby for security, I ran the electric clippers on low. Then I moved closer and closer until Scout became used to the sound. When that was going well, I let him feel the buzzing appliance against his flanks. By the time he was ready for a proper grooming, he had no fear of the clippers.

When he wasn't playing, Scout began general training. A young foal's attention span is short, so Jorge and I conduct many brief sessions. We taught Scout to walk on a lead line close to his handler, much like heeling for a dog. Jorge and I use pats and love as rewards. We keep training light and positive to build a natural trust and rapport.

"Can they high-five or roll over?" a little boy once asked when he met the horses.

I smiled. Many youngsters expect to see the horses perform. "No, we don't teach our horses tricks," I replied. "All of the training we do is about safety." I made a motion and said a few words, and the horse walked forward, then stopped. I had the horse back up and stand in a certain location.

"Ah!" the children said, understanding.

The next step for Scout was getting used to being inside our house while his mom grazed outside the open door. She had every opportunity to come inside too if she wanted, but I always surmised that she was happy to get a break from her frisky foal! Scout practiced his footing on the textured kitchen tiles and the soft living room carpet. I led him through doors and down narrow hallways. Sometimes Jorge snuggled with him on the sofa and watched TV. Little Scout loved being indoors. For him, the absolute most fun of anything was exploring our house. It wasn't uncommon for Jorge and me to see a horse or two standing on our porch, peeking in the windows. Sometimes they even moved from window to window to get a better view of us as we moved from room to room inside. But Scout took it one step further. If there was a way to get inside, he would. His curiosity knew no limits.

One afternoon I walked into the living room to find Scout with his nose poked inside my pocketbook. When I scolded him, he looked up like a kid caught with his hand in the cookie jar, then took off running through the house. *Wheee! I'm having fun!* he seemed to say. He grabbed a floppy fleece dog toy and ran off with it. "Scout, give the dog back his toy." But no, the little horse scooted out the open door. From then on, whether it was a ball, a bone, or a braided rope, Scout made a game of stealing the dog's toys.

When he was a month old, we took Scout, along with Wakanda, for a brief training session at the local rehab hospital. It was always exciting for the patients to see the baby horses. Jorge lifted Scout, barely twenty pounds at the time, and carried him inside. A monitor beeped. Scout looked around, curious but calm. Jorge gave Scout the opportunity to walk on the gleaming tiles. Inside and outside, a hospital may have up to ten different surfaces for the horses to master. We led Scout through the sliding automatic doors, and he peeked at his reflection in the shiny glass. Nothing seemed to faze him.

Another day we took Scout to the medical building next to the rehab hospital to get used to the elevators. Eventually he'd learn to ride inside, but we would take it gradually. First, we'd watch the doors open and close. Then we'd walk onto the elevator and right off again. Next, we'd ride the elevator one floor. After that we'd experience getting into a crowded elevator, standing alongside dollies and wheelchairs, and riding next to people with arms full of flowers and balloons.

There is so much a little horse has to learn about working in a hospital, and most of it involves figuring out how to navigate tight spaces. Most of the members of our herd are 25 to 27 inches tall—our horses tend to be on the small side for the breed. Their compact size makes it easier to get around in cramped hospital rooms.

Another skill the horses learn is "leave it." Hanging charts look fun to play with, and food or medication left on a counter may seem like a tempting snack, so a flawless "leave it" command is essential. We also teach the horses to keep their feet back and stretch their neck forward toward the patient to keep from stepping on wires or tubes or toes. But we don't train the horses to put their head on the bed or on a patient's lap. We want the interaction with the patient to be real. If the horses put their head on a patient's lap, they do so on their own. The horses respond to the person, and many possess a natural ability to find the one individual in a crowd who needs them most. That's something that can't be taught.

Scout's training progressed well. One morning I looked over our calendar and thought the time was right for his first official visit. "We're scheduled to go to the library later this week," I told Jorge. "I'd like to take Wakanda and Scout."

"I think it's the perfect time." Jorge nodded in agreement. "I took him and Wakanda into town last week, and he did great."

At three months old, Scout was already adept at walking on a halter alongside his mother around the pasture. We'd also taken him into town many times for socialization. There, he strolled down the sidewalks, met friendly people, and got used to new sounds and smells. He practiced stepping onto a sidewalk, crossing a road, and walking through a parking lot. A horse's tendency is to run away when frightened. Jorge and I teach the horses that, when in public, we are the herd leader and will always protect them. "Of course, everyone wanted to come up and pat him," Jorge said. A miniature horse draws a lot of attention, and a baby miniature horse even more so. Jorge always shows people the right way to approach, so the horses always associate people with a positive experience.

"He's already good at riding in the trailer," I added. Using the same method as when we introduce the horses to elevators, we'd acquainted Scout to the horse trailer. Step one, we walked Scout and Wakanda up to the trailer and opened the door—Scout would always travel with his mother. Step two, we walked them inside the trailer, then right back out. Step three, they stayed for a few minutes in the trailer, making sure it was a pleasant experience. Scout had made it through all the steps with flying colors. "He's not afraid of anything," I said.

The library was close by and would be a great debut for Scout. When we arrived, two volunteers organized the children in rows, and I read a story. "Now," I said, "we have a special treat. Wakanda's baby is here with us today. Would you like to help train him?"

"Yes!" The boys and girls said, excited to help.

"Great! Now, let's all sit still and be very quiet. Scout is fearless, but this is new for him. And see this piece of tape here on the floor? Keep your fingers and toes on the other side of the tape so they don't get stepped on. Okay, here comes Mr. Jorge. Are you ready to help train Scout?"

Jorge led the tiny horse inside, and the children squirmed excitedly. But remembering the rules, they stayed very quiet. "Scout is learning to work inside around a large group, and by being so good and so quiet, you are helping him learn," Jorge said. He stood Scout on a mat and crouched beside him, holding the lead line.

"Does anyone have questions?" I asked.

"Does he bite?" one boy wondered.

"No. Scout trusts us, and he depends on us to never put him in a bad situation, so he doesn't have to worry. We'd never bring a horse out to spend time with you if we thought he'd bite or kick."

"But what if somebody bumped into him?" another child asked.

"Even then. If someone pokes or bumps into one of our horses by accident, the horse will step away. They can tolerate things, but they shouldn't have to. That means that they are trained to be calm and steady in difficult situations, but we also make sure they aren't put in those situations. That's why we put that piece of tape down for you to sit behind. And that's why we have these nice volunteers you see around you, to help make sure everyone sits where they should and treats the horses the way they should."

Another child's hand shot up. I was prepared for the question every child wanted to know. "What if he has to go to the bathroom?" Every child in the room giggled.

"Just like you, the horses know it's best to go before taking a car ride," I said, and the children laughed again. "Mr. Jorge and I always give the horses opportunities before we enter a building, and we take them outside for plenty of breaks too." Our goal is that each horse would never have an accident, and this only happens through a close relationship with them.

We gave a few children turns to pat Scout gently. Scout's little tail swung lightly as he enjoyed the attention. He was doing great. The children left the library feeling like they'd helped train a horse, and Scout left having succeeded in his first big outing.

The following week Scout was ready for another new adventure. Outside the local rehab hospital there's a beautiful mobility garden. This courtyard of flowers and shrubs is surrounded by steps, curbs, bridges, and ramps. There's soft grass, bumpy cement, benches, and obstacles. The patients can relearn how to walk or use their wheelchairs on the different surfaces, building skills for daily living. When Jorge was a young boy, he'd had to face a lengthy hospitalization after he was hit by a car. He told me that he would have loved having a friendly animal to encourage him. So that's one reason we enjoy bringing the horses to the mobility garden to help patients in rehab.

This garden is also an excellent place for our young horses to learn to navigate various surfaces. And now it was Scout's turn. As he entered, I noticed a woman learning to use a wheelchair. A physical therapist walked beside her, showing her how to use her arm strength to roll the wheels up an incline. Jorge led Scout over to the woman and stood beside her chair. He instructed Scout to slow his pace and stay away from the wheels. At the same time as the woman was learning to use the wheelchair, Scout was learning to walk beside a wheelchair. The woman looked down, reached over, and ruffled Scout's stubbly mane. She was there to get better. And Scout was right by her side.

9

"They're part of the herd."

Everything about the goat farm I was touring that day fascinated me. The picturesque rural setting. The rows of wooden hives housing colonies of bees. The tangle of frisky goats that romped and tumbled across the grass. But what really caught my attention were the animals gathered in the middle of the herd—large, muscular, and alert, with thick white coats.

"Those are our Maremmas," the farmer, whose name was Bob, told me. One glance at the calm and watchful presence of the dogs, and I felt confident I'd found the answer to a problem that had caused a devastating loss on our farm.

101

A month earlier, on a warm March morning, I was in the kitchen when Jorge's frantic shouts sent me flying out to the pasture. I arrived to a ghastly scene of blood everywhere and Jorge rushing our sweet horse Catherine into the trailer. I watched in horror as she thrashed from her injuries. Her best friend, tiny little Mozart, lay dead on the ground. I recoiled in shock. *What had just happened here?*

"Dogs!" Jorge gasped. "They dug under the fence." Although his words were wrought with anger and panic, his actions remained steady and strong. He swung the trailer door closed and jumped in the truck. "I saw it happen. Three dogs came charging into the pasture. The horses scattered, but the dogs got Mozart and Catherine before I could do anything!" I stayed behind, reeling with emotion, while Jorge sped off to the veterinarian. After twenty years of living safely, everything had changed in an instant.

Mozart was gone. And despite two weeks, multiple surgeries, and the veterinarian's heroic efforts, Catherine didn't make it either. I grieved hard, trying to come to terms with the violent loss of two innocent horses, two equine helpers, two companions. I couldn't shake it off. I had to do something.

Friends had suggested guard dogs and even guardian donkeys. Then my friend Sarah called me one night. She is very knowledgeable about dogs. "Have you considered livestock guardian dogs?" she asked. I hadn't. But I did some research, and that's how I came to be at Bob's goat farm that day, on a mission to explore a new way of protecting the horses.

"Maremma Sheepdogs aren't *guard dogs*," Bob said. "They're *livestock guardian dogs*. They bond with the

102

flock—the flock is theirs, not the territory. They're tough and brave. Coyotes, hawks . . . we haven't had a problem since we got them."

"Yes, that's what we need," I said. I'd already told him about Gentle Carousel and the details of our tragic loss.

"To be honest, I don't know of anyone who keeps Maremmas with horses," Bob said. "But I think they'd do great." A retired Navy SEAL, he came across as informed and astute.

"Are they good with people . . . are they friendly?" I asked, eyeing the dogs from safely behind the fence. I wouldn't want guardian dogs who saw us as threats.

"They'll protect you from strangers, but they're very loyal to their family. Still, our Maremmas would rather be with the goats. They're not an inside-the-house, lie-on-the-couch dog. They're part of the herd. They move around with the goats and sleep with the goats."

I nodded, my mind made up. I'd done my research, and I knew these dogs could provide the kind of security we needed for our situation. We were prepared for the extra time and training they'd require. "This is exactly what we need. I'm very interested in your puppies. How much are they?"

Bob rubbed his beard but didn't answer the question. "Why don't you come with me and take a look?" He led me to the barn, where we knelt on the wide floorboards beside a pen of wiggly white balls of fur.

"If I wasn't sold before, I am now!" I said. How could I resist the adorableness before me?

"We have two litters. The older ones are out with their mom and some of the goats. The ones here are still too young to leave their mama. But I'll tell you what." Bob picked up one of the pups and cradled it to his chest. "I like what you're doing with the horses, helping others. I think . . ." he looked thoughtfully at the puppies. "I think these Maremma Sheepdogs were born to do something important. When they're ready, I'll give you two, the pick of each litter." He placed the squirming puppy in my arms. "No charge."

I hugged the puppy, barely able to believe what I had heard, and thanked Bob profusely. Once again, a stranger was extending a totally unexpected kindness to help ensure that our horses could continue their work helping others.

Later, as I relayed the experience to Jorge, I still couldn't believe what had happened. "He's giving us two puppies. He insisted," I said. "They're ours!"

"That's too generous," Jorge said, yet I saw his muscles relax. We'd both be relieved to include such an amazing security presence on the farm. While the fence we had was already sturdy, with wire mesh filling the spaces between the horizontal planks, we took additional steps to reinforce the fencing around the property. We buried barbed wire around the entire perimeter to prevent another animal from digging under. Along the border where the intruder dogs had entered, we erected a double fence. The Maremma Sheepdogs would be yet another defense.

When the older litter was ready, our first puppy arrived, the fuzz around his neck standing up like a lion's mane. I cradled him as I introduced him to each horse. "This is

104

Vigil," I said, holding up the squirmy pup. The horse sniffed the puppy, and Vigil bravely touched her nose with his furry paw. I moved to the next horse, and the next, until the little guy had met them all. "This is Vigil. Meet Vigil." I introduced Vigil to every person, every animal on the farm, and every house pet so he'd know who belonged and who didn't.

Training a livestock guardian dog is unlike training a house pet, and also unlike training a miniature horse. We talked to Bob for hours, and he gave us sound advice, although his experience was with goats, not horses. We studied, researched, and joined Maremma Sheepdog groups online. When we couldn't find others who kept Maremmas with horses, we took all the information we'd gathered and adapted it to our own situation.

The puppies were to be part of the herd, but for many months they wouldn't be left alone with the horses. It was important to keep both the pups and the horses safe. Several times every day, Jorge and I brought Vigil into the barn and let him get used to the horses' smells, whinnies, and snorts, rewarding him with pats and affection. Day after day we walked him along the perimeter of the farm, leading him up to the pasture fence to get close to the horses. "We have to be sure he won't chase them," Jorge said.

Maremma Sheepdogs are different from the other dogs we've had because they're independent thinkers. Two thousand years ago in Italy, they were bred to be left alone with a herd of sheep—they had to make their own decisions. "It's like trying to teach the teacher," I said as Jorge and I practiced training Vigil in the front yard, reinforcing commands such as "down" and "stay." Vigil was an old soul, but puppies will be puppies—even Maremma puppies—and he sometimes got into mischief. He loved to dig a hole and lie in it, then pop his head up to surprise us. Other times he'd relocate a hat or rope or some small tool out into the pasture.

Fortunately, the horses liked Vigil, and the pup soon became calm and comfortable around them. When the second pup, Guardenia, was ready to join us, we followed the same procedure. She was a quick learner, following Vigil's example. The pair bonded nicely with the horses.

At eight months old, the dogs began working independently in the pastures and fields. They moved with the herd during the day and kept watch over them at night. They patrolled the perimeter and barked an alarm if anything approached. One night after we secured the horses and dogs in the inner pasture, Jorge took a look at the GPS trackers we'd attached to the dogs' collars. "They're covering a lot of miles," he said. "I think it's too much work for two dogs." So we searched for more puppies to join the family, and eventually the two protectors grew to a strong and capable team of eight livestock guardian dogs—Vigil, Guardenia, Mirage, Gaia, Halo, Sentrina, Willow, and Sirius.

The dogs did so much for us, so I was always trying to do something for them to enhance their environment. But I kept forgetting how self-sufficient they were. When Vigil and Guardenia first arrived, I bought them sturdy, elevated pet beds and placed them neatly side by side. I pictured the horses relaxing in the barn while the dogs rested comfortably on their attractive new beds. Instead, the dogs slept in the dirt, under the truck, beside a tree . . . basically anywhere but on the beds.

Another time I purchased new, rugged toys for the dogs—durable, power-chewer quality shapes in vibrant colors. I felt like Santa Claus delivering toys to the good and faithful canine boys and girls. But the dogs ran off and found a stick and never once touched the store-bought toys.

On scorching summer days, I thought about the dogs and their heavy coats. They were skilled at adapting to both heat and cold, and we have plenty of shade available in the pasture. We also have misters that provide a cool fog of water droplets. But that year I wanted to do something even more, so I set plastic wading pools out in the pasture, and Jorge filled them with refreshing, cold water. "This is great," I said as we finished the chore. "The Maremmas are going to love these."

Instead, I found them flopped in one of the horses' watering troughs. "You've got perfectly good pools just for you!"

107

I scolded. But you couldn't tell them anything. They did things their own way.

"I guess we know who's in charge," Jorge said, laughing.

Although the dogs were stubborn and independent, I was pleased to see that they were also friendly and affectionate. They ran up to greet me whenever I pulled in the driveway. They liked us, but it was easy to see that they were more attached to the herd. As soon as the dogs said hello to us, they ran back to be with the horses.

As sentinels, Maremma Sheepdogs are barkers. That's how they warn predators and communicate with one another. They have a distinctive call, an alarm they send out when they sense danger. One afternoon I was in the kitchen when I heard the alarm. I rushed outside to find Guardenia cautiously sizing up a Bigfoot garden statue—a joke gift from a friend—that I had set in the corner of the back patio that morning. The observant dog had seen something new in the environment, identified it as some sort of creature, and sensed it as a possible threat. One by one, the other dogs appeared and surrounded the statue. Since Bigfoot didn't provoke them, they simply watched, at the ready. When I gave them the okay, they scattered back to the herd. Is this what would happen, I wondered, if there was a real threat?

One spring evening, as dusk settled around us, I found out. Coyotes howled in the woods. This wasn't the first time I'd heard them. And they weren't only out at night, either—the bold coyotes had also been seen during the day, handily clearing neighbors' five-foot fences to jump into yards. A farmer down the road had chased a coyote from his chicken coop, and another had a coyote take one of his calves. I tensed up every time I heard the eerie calls. That evening the howls drew closer than ever. Jorge and I were working outside when the dogs' alarm bark rang out. "Over there!" Jorge pointed. A coyote was pacing the perimeter. We couldn't see if there were more, but in all likelihood, others weren't far away.

The barking intensified. Powerful white dogs came running from every corner of our property. I watched in amazement as the sentinels fell into line, standing shoulder to shoulder, forming an indomitable barrier. Their fierce barks rang across the pasture. *Don't even think about it. Keep moving.*

For a moment I worried, imagining what would happen if the coyotes didn't heed the warning. I pushed away the images of the brutal attack in the past. *These dogs know what to do*, I reminded myself. *They're strong and capable.* Sure enough, the coyotes turned away. Their howls grew faint. They were not going to challenge the dogs.

The following morning a neighbor called. "Be careful," he said. "We had coyotes up on our front porch last night."

I felt the tension release from my body. We didn't have to worry. We had the Maremmas. We were protected.

10

"You can't change everything, but you can change something."

An overturned car leaned against a fence. A single bare tree stripped of its bark stood in a debris-filled lot. A driveway led to a pile of rubble. After several days of driving (with plenty of rest breaks), Jorge and I had arrived in Moore, Oklahoma. Three miniature horses in the trailer awaited the opportunity to comfort residents of the town ravaged by a powerful tornado.

"This is so different from hurricane damage," I said as we drove through town. A hurricane hit a broad area, but

111

a tornado wound its twisty path, wiping out one side of a street while the other side remained untouched.

Just days earlier, on an ordinary Monday at the end of a routine school day in spring of 2013, an EF5 tornado had ripped through the town (the EF scale ranks the wind speed based on damage, with 5 being the highest). Hundreds of people had been injured and twenty-five were killed, including seven children who were trapped inside an elementary school after the roof collapsed. We had received several emails and phone calls from hospital personnel and families affected by the tragedy, asking if we could come.

We stopped the truck along the side of the road in what had only recently been a thriving neighborhood. It was always difficult emotionally, entering an area of devastation and thinking about the lives affected. A woman sat in a wobbly metal chair amid the remains of her home. A family dug through a pile of broken boards, pulling out books, jackets, bicycles—anything they could salvage. The father held up what appeared to be a photograph, and two sons and a daughter gathered around to see.

We were on our way to connect with several of our volunteers at a nearby farm. The owners had graciously offered to let us and the horses stay there while we were in town. Jorge looked at the families, then back toward the trailer. "Let's just make a quick stop," he said. We opened the doors and stepped out onto the dusty road, then led one of the horses out of the trailer.

The group across the street noticed the activity, dropped their shovels, and hurried over. "What kind of horse is that? Is it a pony? Can I pat it?" the children asked. They patted Sweetheart all over, and Jorge let them help him take her for a short walk. For a while the children laughed. For a while they forgot about the flattened house and missing toys. Their previously sad eyes shone as they gave Jorge high fives. When the family went back to work, they were refueled. Their renewed energy enabled them to dig back into the debris and resume the gritty task of rebuilding their lives.

The next day, Jorge and I met with families whose children had been trapped in the Plaza Tower Elementary School. One father tearfully described how he'd been driving to pick up his child after school, but when he arrived, the school was nothing but a pile of rubble. Tragically, his child hadn't survived. Other families recounted story after story, sharing their grief and trying to conceive how to move forward.

Jorge and I led the horses around to the family members. The horses approached gently, their calmness easing the anxiety in the room. They drew close, allowing each person to lean in, an intimacy that invited trust. The people soon felt the soothing rhythm of patting the soft fur and pressing close to the warm bodies. The horses seemed to understand why they were there. They were interested in people, in tune with emotions. Their piercing blue eyes conveyed that. With some sort of mysterious pull, their soothing allure seemed to draw out the pain and emotions that were at times too difficult to voice.

Midweek, Jorge, Magic, and I arrived at a community center to meet with a group of youngsters who had been in class when the storm hit. They'd huddled in bathrooms, crouching in corners and covering their heads with their backpacks. These students had heard the torrential rain and wind and felt the walls come tumbling down around them. Some of them had been injured. Some had lost friends. I couldn't imagine how they would bear returning to school in the fall.

A crushing sadness filled me. "I wish we could make everything all better," I whispered to Jorge. It was the same desire to fix things that I'd experienced as a young teen when I saw shocking images of starving children on television. I'd sat alone in my living room, watching a commercial featuring hungry babies with bloated, malnourished bellies and empty bowls. I couldn't shake the sight of their deep, sad eyes. After that, each month I sent my hard-earned babysitting money to the Save the Children Fund to sponsor a child from Africa. I wanted to help, but all my babysitting money for six years couldn't change their plight.

Jorge took my arm as we faced that roomful of sad faces. "We'll just do what we can." I remembered what he often said: "You can't change everything, but you can change something."

Magic trotted in to her theme song, "Do You Believe in Magic?" I sat on a folding chair and opened a storybook I'd created. I smiled at the group seated on the floor around me. "Would you like to hear a story about Magic? Do you know that Magic has all different kinds of friends?" I held up the picture of Magic on the first page. "Magic likes small friends and tall friends." I looked around the room. "Raise your hand if you're tall." Several of the children raised their hands. "Who here is small?" Some of the younger children waved their arms in the air. "She likes friends who have long hair," I continued. The group seated around the room began to get the idea, and those with long hair raised their hands. "She likes friends with short hair." The children eagerly responded as I read each page. "Magic likes friends who are happy and friends who are sad." I paused and asked, "Is anyone in this room sad?"

A child raised her hand. Then another. One by one, the children's hands went up until everyone in the room had their arm extended in the air. I looked at the teachers— their hands were raised too. The room fell perfectly quiet, everyone looking around at all the raised hands. The simple act unified them. It was okay to be sad. Everyone was sad.

I swallowed hard. "I tell you what," I said. "Anyone who is sad gets to hug Magic on the way out."

"I'm very, very sad," one boy said.

"Then you get an extra hug," I answered.

After the story, the boys and girls lined up to visit with Magic. They hugged her and talked to her, and she responded to each one with a nuzzle, a gentle touch, or a soft whinny. She likes to be patted and hugged, but I believe she has a sense that she is giving something back as well.

That day we had a tight schedule, and we kept moving so we'd keep on track. Immediately after the community center, the horses were supposed to meet with a young girl who faced the heartbreaking ordeal of attending her friend's funeral. With the horses all packed in the trailer and ready to go, Jorge and I made a quick stop at the hotel to grab some supplies.

When we walked in, the lobby was eerily quiet except for a news broadcast coming from the television. Everyone stood in place, staring at the screen. "Impossible. No way," someone said.

"What's going on?" Jorge asked as he and I exchanged worried glances. Warnings flashed across the TV screen: *Emergency alert! Seek shelter immediately!* I shook my head in disbelief. Only twelve days after the first tornado, a second, even more powerful tornado had changed direction and was heading toward Moore.

In addition, the hotel had no storm shelter for the horses. "Find a place in the hall and cover yourselves with a mattress," the staff urged their guests. Jorge and I shook our heads. This didn't feel like a safe situation to us. We had to get out of there—fast. Our best bet was to jump in the truck and make a run for it.

We started driving, and the skies darkened as if a heavy blanket was being thrown over us. On the highway, roaring winds chased after us. The road became packed with cars, all getting out of town. Lights flashed in the distance; leaves and branches swirled in the sky. A huge dark funnel cloud moved closer. I looked out the side mirror just in time to see a car behind us being lifted by the wind and flipped over. Jorge stepped on the gas. I glanced at a monitor on the dashboard that allows us to view the horses in the trailer. They were casually munching hay. They were calm, even with the thundering noise of a tornado.

I don't know how long we drove outrunning that storm. When it finally felt safe, we pulled into a truck stop and waited. The skies lightened and the roaring winds settled.

"It came so close." I tried to catch my breath.

"But we kept ahead," Jorge said, taking my hand in his and pulling me close.

"Now what?" I asked. I don't like detours—not on the road and not in life. I like to be organized. I like to have a system. But at the moment all our plans were out the window. We were now miles away from Moore. But we still had work to do.

"We have to go back," we agreed. A little girl was counting on us.

However, returning along the same route where a tornado had just passed proved impossible. The highway was clogged with debris, resulting in road closures and detours. The radio kept us apprised of the traffic conditions, as well as the dire statistics: "Winds peaked at 250 miles per hour. The path of destruction is nearly two and a half miles wide. Death toll—six . . . eight . . . nine."

Somehow we were able to snake our way back, arriving in Moore hours later. I could barely believe it was the same town we'd left earlier that day. Power lines were down and roads were flooded. The gas station where we had filled up that morning was nothing but a pile of shredded wood and twisted metal. And our hotel—a section of the roof had caved in, and parts of the siding were ripped off. Trees were missing their tops, and the awning was lying in the muddy, decimated parking lot. What would have happened if we had stayed? Was everyone who did stay okay? And how would all the people in this town, already in the midst of trying to recover from a tornado, handle getting battered by another one? How would they pick up the pieces? How would they ever feel safe again?

We couldn't change *everything*, I reminded myself. But we could do something.

When we're dealing with something huge, like hurricanes and tornadoes, there are times when I wonder if it's enough. We can't rebuild houses. We can't heal injured children. But as I watch our horses trot into a room, I remind myself that what we do matters. How could I ignore the smiles and the tears, the heartfelt requests for us to return? How could I deny the hurting child who met the horses and laughed for the first time in weeks? Or the girl who said thinking of our horses helped her sleep through the night again?

I'll never forget the young boy in hospice care who was very near the end. He'd been in the hospital much of his life—he'd never been home for a holiday, never been to a birthday party or a ball game. But when the doctors and nurses found out that our horses were at the Ronald McDonald House next door, they bundled up the boy and packed up all his medical gear to give him one memorable outing. He spent the afternoon hugging and patting the horses, smiling and laughing. Although he grew tired, he never gave in to the fatigue. Before we left, his mother looked at me, a tear sliding down her cheek. "We've never had a happy day," she said. She turned and hugged Magic. "Now we will always have a happy day."

We can't fix everything. But in those tougher moments, it helps to know that we can do something positive.

In Moore, we made new arrangements with the girl we had planned to visit, connecting with her and her family in a parking lot that hadn't been damaged. Magic trotted right up and laid her head against the girl's cheek. She hugged the horse tightly. When they started on their walk together, the girl ran her hand through Magic's mane. They moved slowly, yet each step they took together was another step forward, another step toward healing. Somehow, I trusted, Magic would give the girl the strength she needed to get through the difficult days ahead.

11

"I hope you dance."

The gray-haired woman in the wheelchair appeared uninterested in the horse we brought to the memory unit that day. She sat there, quietly smoothing her floral-print blouse. When it came her turn to meet the horse, she looked up with a weak smile. "Would you like to say hello?" I asked.

She didn't answer. The horse reached forward and leaned her snowy-white head over the arm of the woman's wheelchair.

"Would you like to pat her?"

No response.

"Her name is Sweetheart."

At that, the woman blinked and caught her breath, as if it was the first time she noticed the horse that was practically in her lap. Her eyes opened wide. The detached smile now connected. "Sweetheart?" She threw her arms out and caressed the horse. "Let me call you Sweetheart," she sang in a soft, warm voice, "I'm in love with you." She went on to sing the old ballad in its entirety, swaying as if rocking the horse. I wondered if in her younger years she had sung that song to her own sweetheart, or maybe to soothe a child. Sweetheart nuzzled gently as she was being serenaded.

The tender closeness between the two made me melt. Just a mention of the name "Sweetheart" had unlocked a memory—or maybe just an emotion—that spoke to the woman. And her responding through music was something I'd seen many times before. Doctors and therapists recognize the value of music for Alzheimer's patients. Those who have trouble recalling the day of the week and names of their relatives often sing along when golden oldies are played, remembering every word of a favorite hymn or a song from their past.

One time the staff at a day program for people with Alzheimer's brought in a piano player. The audience smiled and clapped to the music as we brought the horses around. Another time Aladdin, Cloudburst, and Wakanda were invited to a sock hop at an assisted living center. We love using costumes to help create a mood, so a volunteer sewed old-fashioned poodle skirts for the fillies, and Aladdin wore a blanket designed to look like a leather jacket and jeans. As we walked down the halls to greet the residents, we played the fifties tune "I Found My Thrill on Blueberry Hill." Suddenly

120

doors started to open and the residents came out of their rooms to join the fun. Even those in wheelchairs paraded along with the music as the horses led everyone to the hop.

I've always had an interest in the way music can be used to enrich activities. I began using music when I was a teacher as a way to help calm and settle my students. In the mornings, the boys and girls would enter the classroom to the strains of classical music, signaling a transition from the busy, noisy hallway to a peaceful place of learning. Some of my students were children with disabilities and were already exposed to music therapy. They found it soothing at times, such as when they were overstimulated. I also combined music with my academic themes. If we were studying the ocean, I'd play relaxation music with sounds of waves. For a unit on the rain forest, I found music with waterfalls and birdsong. The students came to ask for this and even suggested songs they knew that fit the study topics.

Recalling the positive responses of my students, I started incorporating music in our Gentle Carousel events. We play upbeat numbers to signify something exciting is about to begin and also when we're done to let people know it's time to get ready to go. The right song always adds polish to an event and helps fill in time when we transition to a new activity or changing horses to give each one a break. We're always learning what type of music speaks to different people. Some children in the hospital enjoy bouncy pop songs, while others prefer relaxing piano music and soft ballads. Music not only helps relax people but it also seems to help put them in a good mood.

That's how I got the idea to play a theme song for each horse. Whenever we go to events, each horse is always introduced with his or her song. Most of the horses know their particular tune. When I play Rainbow's song "Somewhere Over the Rainbow," Magic just stands beside me calmly. But when I play her song, "Do You Believe in Magic," she lifts her head, pricks up her ears, and shuffles her front feet, ready to go. Sometimes we introduce the horses with a

current popular song. Once when we were visiting patients at the Monroe Carell Jr. Children's Hospital at Vanderbilt University in Nashville, Tennessee, we played Justin Timberlake's hit song "Can't Stop the Feeling." The children couldn't get enough of it, especially when he sang, "Dance, dance, dance!" and a little horse trotted into the room.

Instead of taking the horses around the wards, we visited patients via the hospital's Seacrest Studios. Monroe Carell Jr. Children's Hospital is one of several prominent urban hospitals that boasts one of these exciting performing arts studios established by the Ryan Seacrest Foundation. It features state-of-the-art radio and television equipment and broadcasts directly into the patients' rooms. Children who are too ill to get out of bed can enjoy live entertainment created just for them. More mobile children can also spend time in the studios, as part of the audience. Celebrities often show up to put on shows for the patients. The studio is lined with portraits of the famous people who have performed there, and Magic's portrait is hanging right alongside country stars such as Taylor Swift and Rascal Flatts!

Other hospitals also have studios and stages where we play music and read books. Once, a performance director arranged a question-and-answer television show with us. They provided a wonderful host for the show, and we brought along Magic, Sunshine, and Dream. We sat around a desk with microphones and monitors. I'm usually coordinating events and taking pictures, or speaking in front of audiences at large events. Jorge is our go-to guy for interviews, so we decided that he'd answer the questions. Some young patients sat in the audience, while others would call in from their rooms. *Lights! Camera! Action!*

"Okay, who has a question for Mr. Jorge?" the host asked.

Right away, the phone rang. "Hello, this is Jenny from the sixth floor. What are the horses' names?"

"Jenny wants to know what the horses' names are," the host repeated, and Jorge responded.

A boy seated in the audience asked a question, and then the phone rang again. "Hello, this is Jenny from the sixth floor. I want to know, how old are they?"

Jorge smiled and provided the answer.

After another few questions, the phone rang again. "Hello, this is Jenny from the sixth floor. What do your horses like to eat?"

Jorge stifled a laugh and told Jenny what the horses like to eat. After she rang in a fourth time, he whispered to me, "We've got to send some surprises up to Jenny on the sixth floor!" We put together a stuffed horse and a few books, along with a hoof-a-graphed note telling her how much we appreciated her interest and hoped she'd get well soon.

In addition to visiting the children's hospital, we had been asked to participate in a major charity fundraising concert for MusiCares, an organization featuring popular country music singers. We visit Nashville several times a year, and we love the warm, friendly city, so we were thrilled for the chance to be onstage at the famous Franklin Theatre and help out a good cause.

We drove past the historic red-and-gold marquee and parked our trailer behind the building. Freshly bathed and with his pure white mane and tail fluffed up from a good brushing, Prince followed us inside the beautifully restored old theater. He walked along, eager and confident, yet he looked so tiny in that big venue.

We were met by a stage manager who asked if he could get us anything. "Could we do a quick run-through?" Jorge asked. We'd been told that all we were expected to do was to walk out on stage, meet the crowd, and wave hello. It sounded simple enough, but we never put the horses in an unfamiliar situation without practice. We wanted to give Prince a chance to get comfortable with the new surroundings and learn what to expect. The stage manager showed us where we'd wait and gave us some more specifics. "You'll come in this way," he said, pointing toward a hallway already jammed with sound and lighting people. "Here's the stage entrance. Feel free to check it out."

Jorge led Prince out onto the stage. A band was playing, and an artist stood behind a floor mic, rehearsing her song. Jorge and Prince walked around, faced the rows with hundreds of seats and the balcony way in the back, and looked at the lights and sound equipment. After they'd taken it all in, they returned backstage.

"I showed him the curtains and the lights and everything," Jorge said.

"Okay, we're good," I said.

Every seat in the theater was filled when the thick, purple curtains parted. I stood in the wings where I could watch as Jorge and Prince were introduced. The announcer explained what our organization was all about and mentioned our work with families at Sandy Hook Elementary School. "All the way from Florida, please welcome Gentle Carousel's Priiiiiiince!"

The applause started soft, then rose. As soon as Prince came into view, the audience broke out in unison, "Awwww." Tiny Prince hurried along beside Jorge. The clapping and cheering grew until it became the loudest thundering applause I'd ever heard. The whole audience jumped to their feet, clapping and cheering. We'd prepared for the stage and the lights and the music and everything we could think of, but a standing ovation? Prince had never been exposed to such commotion, but he simply nodded his head and took it all in like a champ.

"Prince was so calm and cool!" I told Jorge when they returned backstage. "I think he likes showbiz."

Before we left, we listened to Grammy-winning songwriter Tia Sillers performing the number one song she wrote for LeeAnn Womack, "I Hope You Dance." The beginning of the song is about how life can fill us with wonder. The words swirled around me—I was filled with wonder that this tiny little horse trusted us enough to confidently follow us onstage at a large and noisy music venue. That all the horses trusted us in so many situations that were new and different. Did I trust as much? How much faith did I have when put in difficult situations?

The song goes on to say that we shouldn't take one single breath for granted. That line nudged at me too. I thought of the children we'd just visited in the hospital, some of them struggling for their next breath. How could anyone take it for granted? How could I?

Then Tia's beautiful voice came to the chorus, the inspiration for the title. The message is that when given the opportunity of either sitting back without taking a risk or dancing, "I hope you dance."

That was it, wasn't it? There are times in life that are challenging, times that are painful. There are times when everything feels like too much to handle. But that's just the time to dig deep and find our strength. That's the message we hope our horses bring to the people we visit.

Gather your courage. Take a step. There's still hope.

And that's the message I would keep here in my heart for whenever I feel anxious and afraid. *I hope you dance.*

12

"We'll always have this day."

Although I knew by the calendar that it was December 25, 2016, it didn't feel like Christmas. We were in Gatlinburg, Tennessee, the gateway to Great Smoky Mountains National Park. With just one main road down the center of town, the small resort area attracted millions of tourists each year to enjoy the hiking and scenic attractions, as well as shops, distilleries, amusement parks, and museums.

That year heavy winds had swept wildfires down from the mountains and through the town. Seventeen thousand acres of land were destroyed, and more than two thousand homes and businesses burned to the ground. Flames forced fourteen thousand people to flee their homes. Tragically, fourteen people lost their lives, and nearly two hundred more were injured.

We arrived several weeks after the fires, but the effects were still pronounced—bare trees, collapsed buildings, abandoned cars. We passed people picking through the charred rubble of their homes, hoping to find something to salvage. It was never easy to see such loss. I glanced up at the dashboard monitor that showed the horses in the trailer. I knew they were along to encourage the hurting people of the town, but seeing them there in the trailer, swinging their heads and casually munching their hay, always brought me comfort as well.

We stopped to see as many displaced families as possible. Some were staying with friends, while others camped out in the lobby of one of the big hotels that had not been damaged. Everywhere we went I felt the positive spirit of the community—all I heard was concern for others and offers of help. Scout, Magic, and Sweetheart made the rounds. I was moved by how warmly everyone treated them and how happy they were that we had come.

Late afternoon we pulled into a parking lot where a group of men labored in the brisk air to clean up some landscaping. When we led the horses out of the trailer, the men paused, leaning on their shovels and rakes. They took their time ruffling the horses' manes and marveling at their miniature size. As we chatted, the thing that impressed me, as it often did in these situations, was their optimistic attitude. "We're going to rebuild," said a man wearing heavy gloves and a baseball cap. "We just want to be able to work." They didn't want handouts; they didn't ask for anything.

They just pulled themselves up by the bootstraps and got to business—thinking of others, helping when they could, and keeping positive. We stayed for a while longer, then let them get back to work.

After our visit, we were sitting in the parking lot while Jorge checked a map on his cell. I had just closed my eyes to relax for a moment when I heard a tap at the window. A small group of men and women stood in a cluster with little ones hanging on the parents' arms. I rolled down the window, assuming they would ask to see the horses. I was tired, but of course we'd get out and let them say hello. But the people just smiled and then began to lift their voices in song.

"Silent night, holy night, all is calm, all is bright." They caroled to us right there by the street, the sincere harmonies working their way straight to my weary heart. Christmas had arrived after all. No tragedy would stop it. As the holiday spirit blanketed us, Jorge slid his arm around my shoulders. After the caroling, one of the women leaned in and said, "We just want to thank you for all you're doing for us." I was touched—with everything they had to deal with, they had taken time to express gratitude for our efforts.

That night we stopped at a restaurant for dinner, parking the trailer by the window so we could keep watch. It wasn't very busy, but I noticed three young children—about ages six to nine—alone at a table in the back. It appeared that they'd been there for a while, as they worked with paper and crayons to keep themselves busy. Occasionally a waitress, who I assumed was their mother, took time to talk with them, bring them snacks, and refill their beverages. When I inquired, I learned that they were sitting at that table because they'd lost their home and had no place to go while their families were busy working in the restaurant. Here it was Christmas, and these children had no presents, no tree, nothing to bring them cheer. They were stuck inside for hours at a restaurant table without their parents for company. Jorge and I exchanged a glance, the kind that meant we wanted to try to help.

I approached the children and smiled. "I was just wondering if you might like to come and meet our horses," I said, "with your parents' permission."

The children looked at each other, eyes wide, and scrambled to their feet. After I explained to the parents, we all went outside to the parking lot and Jorge opened the trailer doors. "Here's Magic and Scout and Sweetheart."

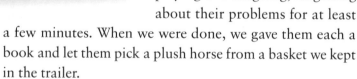

"They're so small!" the boy said.

"They're so cute!" the girls exclaimed together.

We led Magic out of the trailer, and they stroked her long mane. We answered all their questions, then Jorge accompanied each child with a turn walking Magic around the parking lot. They were so happy, playing and laughing, forgetting about their problems for at least a few minutes. When we were done, we gave them each a book and let them pick a plush horse from a basket we kept in the trailer.

"Oh, I love this red one," the boy said, making his selection.

"Is there one with flowers?" the youngest asked, and the three sorted through the basket until they found her one. When they'd each selected their horse and dashed off to show

130

their parents in the restaurant, I felt as if we'd given them each the most coveted gift from Santa's sleigh.

As we got in the truck and pulled around, I looked through the restaurant window and picked out the children's table in the back. They were laughing and smiling, trotting their horses around the tabletop, walking them into makeshift barns of folded menus, jumping them over sugar bowls. These children had lost everything, yet our simple gifts brought them a few moments of happiness in a difficult time. We drove away feeling much merrier than we had before.

We do our best to help make Christmas a magical holiday wherever we go. I make an effort to plan creative touches such as dressing the horses in holiday outfits. Sometimes they wear a red coat with white Santa trim, or a green cape, or blue blankets and matching halters adorned with white embroidery and silver glitter. One of our favorite places to visit, the Ronald McDonald House of North Central Florida, celebrates Christmas twice a year: once in December, and in the hopes of giving every child a chance to experience the joys of the holiday, they also have Christmas in July. Ronald McDonald House is a home away from home for very ill children and their families. When a child is admitted to the hospital, this residence offers parents and siblings a nearby place to stay so that they can be on hand to comfort and support the child. Sometimes the child stays in the house with the rest of the family and shuttles back and forth to the hospital for daily treatments. Whenever we travel to any event, we always arrange to stop at a nearby Ronald McDonald House.

Nearly all of our horses had been to the Ronald McDonald House of North Central Florida on multiple occasions. The sprawling facility accommodates as many as twenty-five families at a time, with separate bedrooms, a large living room, playgrounds, and a butterfly garden—a peaceful outdoor park with paths for walking and benches for resting. This is where we like to offer children the opportunity to walk the horses, which is often enough to motivate reluctant patients to get out of bed and get some fresh air and exercise.

One year we arrived for the Christmas in July celebration. The organizers asked if we'd let one of our horses ride up to the building in a car with Ronald McDonald himself. If you go to clown school, landing a part as Ronald McDonald is one of the most prestigious jobs you can obtain. With his classic red wig, red nose, and bright yellow jumpsuit, he makes most youngsters—even those who are a little afraid of clowns—squeal with delight. Riding in a car with Ronald would be like sitting next to Santa Claus in the Macy's Thanksgiving Day parade.

When we arrived at the designated spot with Rainbow at the ready, there was Ronald wearing his elaborate costume—he was so tall, and his clown shoes were nearly as long as Rainbow! I could barely believe that this bigger-than-life character was sitting inside the tiniest clown car I'd ever seen. Jorge and I laughed as we settled Rainbow in the passenger seat of the minuscule convertible. We walked alongside as the minicar putted slowly down the driveway. "Look!" said Ronald. "Do you like my car?" He pointed to Rainbow. "It's one horsepower!"

We helped Rainbow out of the car and met Santa, who was decked out in his summer outfit—a traditional Santa hat, tropical shirt, and red shorts. Railings were decorated with garlands and lights, and there was even a child-sized model train running around the parking lot. An adorable girl dashed right up to Rainbow and followed us into the house. I was aware that this little girl wasn't feeling well, yet she lit up with joy whenever she saw the horses arrive. Her mother told me that on the days she wasn't feeling her best, she'd fold her arms across her chest and tell the doctors she'd only get out of bed for the horses. She always spoke right to the horses—"Are you okay? Are you happy?"

That Christmas in July the girl was beaming. She was on cloud nine with all the holiday celebrations and being with the horses. "I'm glad Christmas has come early this year," her mother said softly. I heard in her voice an unspoken sadness. "No matter what, we'll always have this day." The child settled herself on a pillow under the sparkling Christmas tree in the living room. Rainbow nuzzled up against her, and she threw her arms around him. I smiled in that moment. It's an image that stays in my mind.

Many long-term patients get to know us so well that they want to be our helpers. One preteen boy, Austin, loved helping us, and I saw what a difference it made in his recovery. "When I get better, I'm going to be one of your volunteers," Austin told us on one of our visits. The next time we came, we brought him a black wool driving cap, just like the one Jorge always wears, and an ID badge on a lanyard. "You're an honorary volunteer now," I said, slipping the badge over his head. "How would you like to help us out today?" Austin pulled himself up, threw his shoulders back, and followed us outside. He helped open the trailer doors and watched Jorge bring the horses down the ramp. He proudly showed the younger kids how to walk with the horses just as he had done many times himself. Being able to help rather than being the one to receive help gave this young man purpose as he braved his cancer treatments. He still had a long battle. The

day he left for home, Austin turned and waved goodbye. "I'll be back to volunteer," he said, "when I get better." Sadly, he did not get better. But we are so thankful he had that day to live out his dream of volunteering with us before he died.

Although we often visit hospitals and Ronald McDonald Houses on holidays, not all of our Christmases are difficult and sad. We love outfitting the horses with reindeer antler headbands and making children laugh. We've taken part in holiday fundraisers for charitable causes, where goodwill overflows. One year Magic was invited to act in one performance of the classic holiday ballet *The Nutcracker*. The national tour was scheduled to play at the Curtis M. Phillips Center for the Performing Arts in Gainesville, Florida, and they had arranged an adaptation of the show called "The Magic of *The Nutcracker*." For that performance, Magic was cast as the Sugar Plum Fairy. The organizers invited students from the Florida School for the Deaf and Blind who would be able to interact with the show by using their other senses—for instance, they could touch the costumes and sit up on the stage to feel the vibrations of the dance steps.

The costumers sewed Magic a beautiful pink outfit with a poufy tutu and fitted her with an elegant silver tiara. "She's dressed just like us!" the ballerinas chirped. This would be one of Magic's first times on a stage without us right by her side, but Jorge stayed within her line of sight. She was perfectly comfortable, even with some of the strange goings-on around her. She merely watched as an actor played the larger-than-life Mother Ginger, who was taller than anyone Magic had ever seen before. I was surprised when a flurry of young ballerinas came spilling out from behind Mother Ginger's wide skirts and pirouetting around, but Magic kept playing her part without a hitch.

I never thought Magic would perform in a ballet, but it helped some students with different needs to experience the production in a special way. Seeing Magic onstage with a cast of professional dancers and ballerinas is something I'll never forget. I carry it with me, and when times are challenging, no matter if it's Christmas or any other time of year, that magical holiday feeling settles over me. I know that there are surprises awaiting me in life—surprises as magnificent as a miniature equine Sugar Plum Fairy in a tutu.

13

"In the worst of times, we see the best in people."

We've dealt with both natural and man-made disasters, and it always saddens me to see people facing such hardships. Hurricanes. Fires. Crime. Violence. Terrorism. Tragedy is a sad, somber reality. Yet, in these times, we always find examples of the goodness of humanity. It can't make up for the horrors and the lives lost. But we have to grasp what hope we can find when we go into a place of tragedy.

In 2015, news erupted of a horrific mass shooting at the Emanuel African Methodist Episcopal Church in Charleston,

South Carolina. What happened at the church that day shocked us all. A young man entered the sanctuary during a Bible study, talked with a few of the worshipers, and then opened fire, leaving nine dead, including the pastor. A family member of one of the victims called Gentle Carousel the day after the shooting. Would we bring the horses? Could we come right away?

Jorge and I quickly arranged the details and made the daylong trip. When we arrived, the community was overflowing with mourners, government officials, and news media. It wasn't easy squeezing the bulky horse trailer down the narrow Charleston streets. "We're not going to fit," I said, cringing as we inched along. We had to park blocks from the church and walk the horses through street after congested street.

Hundreds of bereaved men, women, and children gathered on the sidewalk and flowed out into the road in front of the stately white stucco church. Camera crews and reporters pressed in and stood beside the massive wreaths and memorials. Jorge and I didn't enter the packed church but waited off to the side amid the throng so we would be available for the funeral-goers before and after the services. The intense heat equaled the Florida sun, but we were well prepared with water and fans. Magic, Dream, and Rainbow stood in the shade awaiting the crowds. People on the street continued flooding forth, bringing flowers and holding vigil as the services continued inside the church.

As people flowed out the doors after the service, a petite older woman approached us. She wore a long black dress with a lace collar and fancy embroidery, and a beautiful wide-brimmed hat topped with curled veiling and little silver pearl beads. The woman only had eyes for Magic. "Oh my goodness, aren't you precious?" Right there on the sidewalk, in her elegant funeral attire, she bent down on her knees to go eye-to-eye with the little horse. "You're beautiful, baby." She hugged Magic tight, almost unwilling to let go. It seemed as if they exchanged a compassionate moment before she stood up, proud and strong. "You should be over there," she said with emphasis, pointing to the swarm near the steps of the church. "That's where all the TV people are. You need to go out where the cameras are so they can see you."

"We didn't come to be on TV," I said gently. "Don't you know? We came for you."

The woman stared. "Me?" She dabbed at her eyes, but the tears flowed anyway from the emotional day—and now the unexpected comfort of a tiny horse with a shiny black mane. "God bless you," she said.

Many others approached us that day, surprised to find the little horses, and their hearts were a little lighter after spending time together. "There is darkness in the world," a man said, "but there is goodness here in these horses."

The next day we were asked to attend the memorial service for the church's pastor, Reverend Clementa Pinckney. It was held at the packed TD Arena at the College of Charleston, where thousands gathered to pay their respects. It was clear that he was a beloved pastor, a respected man, and an influential state senator. The stadium filled, as well as the viewing areas in adjacent buildings and every place in between. Traffic backed up and other roads closed due to the arrival of President Obama, who would deliver the eulogy.

That day the speeches were full of words about God's grace and the amazing spirit of the community. My heart went out to all the members of the prayer group who had opened their doors and welcomed a stranger—a stranger who turned against them in violence. How could the parishioners ever have imagined the devastating outcome of their act of kindness and love? Yet, over and over throughout our visit, I saw the grace and love in the community as they moved forward in faith.

I couldn't change what had happened, and I couldn't heal broken hearts. I only knew how to do one thing: bring the horses and offer compassion. And every time my heart felt heavy, it was instantly lifted again when I saw the hope that our horses brought. I saw hope when an elegant woman got down on her knees to wrap her arms around Magic. I saw hope when a solemn man let down his guard and broke into tears. I saw hope when a group of children flocked around us and smiled. I saw hope when a rugged first responder gently hugged a tiny horse. This place was overflowing with hope.

During the week we spent in Charleston, we visited the Ronald McDonald House and were guests at an event to support first responders. I was renewed by the goodness of everyone we met. Jorge and I sat across from each other over dinner the night before we left town. "There is so much strength in the people here. A strong faith," I said. This community reflected grace and forgiveness under horrible circumstances. "It must take so much courage to find forgiveness after such tragedy. I'll never cease to be amazed. In the worst of times, we see the best in people."

Before we left, we were invited to a picnic by members of a church. We thought we were there to serve them, but once again the community doted on us. Some people made sure the horses were comfortable in the shade, and children brought them water. We were served delicious sandwiches and fresh fruit. "What can we do for you?" they asked. "Is there any way we can help?" Their love was a blessing, and the picnic was a wonderful way to shake it off.

My feelings were mixed as we drove home. I knew inexplicable tragedies would continue to happen. There would always be the need for comfort, peace, and healing. Given the nature of our work, we are constantly exposed to ill children, grieving families, patients experiencing their final breaths—and, sadly, acts of violence.

Yet we had a little blessing in store for us at home. While we were in Charleston, our caretaker back at the farm had informed us that one of our mares was ready to foal. We were disappointed to miss the birth but knew she would be in good hands. When we got home, we met the little sorrel filly with white stockings on her legs. We watched the adorable foal nurse, the mother turning to gently nuzzle her baby. Her arrival was so joyful, and it was just what I needed—a new life, a new beginning.

"I'm going to let the people of Charleston give her a name," I said. I put out a notice on social media asking for suggestions. Before long, the townspeople responded.

They named her Amazing Grace.

14

"It's the real Jorge!"

I tugged at a prickly bale of hay in the back of the truck. Jorge reached in and helped heft the bale. Together we unloaded the truck and filled the back of our all-terrain vehicle to prepare for the morning feeding. It was a physical task, and I was glad to have Jorge beside me. And it wasn't the first time I was grateful that he was my partner in life and in this venture.

While I grew up finding ways to be around animals, Jorge didn't. His family wasn't partial to house pets. Yet Jorge is as invested in our work and as bonded with the horses as I am. I witness this in his gentle ways—the tender care he gives the horses and the respect with which he treats them. But I'm most in awe of his compassion and

143

the way he connects with the people. Although he has his MBA and has worked in business, he's also served as a youth minister and has a heart for helping those in need.

I remember one time when we had just finished a difficult visit at the Ronald McDonald House. One of the patients, a young boy, had passed away, and the other children, who had become his friends, were sad. We stayed an extra-long time to make sure each one got a turn with the horses. After we'd packed everything up and walked the horses into the trailer, I was tending to last-minute business when I noticed Jorge sitting on the curb outside with a man—the boy's father.

The man's wife and family were back home in Mexico, and he didn't have a family member to console him in his bleakest hour. Jorge had noticed him there alone, got out of the truck, and quietly sat beside him. The man didn't speak any English. Jorge was born in Cuba, and although he's lived in the United States most of his life, he still knows a little Spanish. So he communicated with the father as best he could. The grieving man shared stories about his son and how special he was, and Jorge listened. The two men sat together on the curb on that sad day. Nothing could change what the father had lost, but Jorge's little act of kindness helped him get through that one difficult, sad moment and move on to face the next.

Another time, Austin, our honorary volunteer at the Ronald McDonald House, was having a birthday, and we came up with a fun way to celebrate. We knew that Austin loved fire trucks. A friend of ours is a retired firefighter who owns a classic rig, so we arranged to have him give Austin and his father a ride. Our friend even got permission to use the lights and sirens. On the big day we brought Circus, our horse who is white with black spots, much like a Dalmatian. When we arrived, Austin was ready for his ride, but his father wasn't feeling well. "My dad can't go with me," he said sadly.

"Would it be okay if I rode with you?" Jorge asked.

Austin perked up instantly. "Let's go!"

I stayed behind with Circus while Jorge and Austin climbed into the fire truck, grinning from ear to ear. It was clear how much it meant to the boy that Jorge stepped up and filled in when his father couldn't go. Besides, I don't know who had more fun riding in that fire truck, Austin or Jorge.

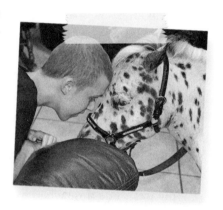

One summer we attended a literacy event at a library on a Saturday afternoon. Jorge moved Moonshadow in a semicircle before a roomful of eager children. When he was done, he got down on one knee to talk to the group. I'd noticed him doing this with the horses too. He always crouched down to be face-to-face with them. No one had ever suggested that he do this; he just knew that children and horses respond better when he communicates with them at their level.

"Let's all say hello to Moonshadow," Jorge said.

The boys and girls all said hello. A boy raised his hand. "Mr. Jorge, how does Moonshadow say hello?"

"That's a good question," Jorge said. "He might whinny or neigh. When horses are out in the pasture, they sometimes greet each other by standing nose to nose and blowing air at each other."

I love watching the way Jorge relates to the boys and girls. I frequently read to the children, but other times I'm focused on dealing with administrators or overseeing the details and making sure everything runs smoothly. Jorge, along with our many volunteers, is usually holding one of the lead lines, guiding the horses and making some sort of presentation to the gathering. For the most part, we try to remain as anonymous as possible. We want people to remember the horses, not us. At the beginning, we didn't use our names in publicity or on our social media. But as we became more involved, people got to know us better and started calling us by name—particularly Jorge.

Since I was usually the one with the camera and Jorge was the one in the pictures we posted, he gained a certain amount of fame. When we went to the bank or post office, a clerk would invariably grin at him and say, "I know who you are!" The time when we were in Sandy Hook, we were talking with an officer at the police station. Jorge was standing beside her, holding Magic's lead, when the officer asked, "Can I have a hug?" Jorge prepared for the woman to bend down and hug Magic. Instead, she swooped in and gave Jorge a big squeeze! He couldn't have been more surprised.

After a while it became difficult for us to remain behind the scenes. Most of the time the attention is flattering, if also a bit baffling. On a recent trip, we pulled our van into a truck stop in North Carolina. The van is wrapped with our Gentle Carousel logo, so it's easily identifiable. A woman in a sedan pulled up behind us and jumped out of her car. "I'm your biggest fan!" she said, running toward the driver's-side window. "I've been following you since the state line, hoping you'd pull over!" It's always surprising when people go out of their way to meet us.

Even when we are far from home, people recognize us. We were doing an event in New York City, driving down the busy Manhattan streets, when we heard a young woman calling from the sidewalk, "Gentle Carousel! I love you!" We couldn't very well stop in the heavy traffic, so Jorge rolled down his window and waved. "Oh my gosh!" the woman squealed, nudging her companion walking beside her. "It's the real Jorge!" After all these years of trying to fade into the background, it surprised Jorge and amused me that people would recognize him from social media and then get excited at seeing him in real life out in public.

Of course, I am lucky enough to know the real Jorge. I can say that he is truly the nicest person I've ever known. He sincerely listens to people and to animals, and sometimes that is all we are really looking for—to be heard. Like most men, he wants to fix anything that is upsetting me. Of course, that is not always possible. When my dog Flynn passed away, I was more distraught than I ever thought I could be, and it was difficult to feel anything but my grief. Flynn was a Shetland sheepdog with beautiful gray, tan, white, and black markings—a coat coloring known as blue merle. I'd had him since he was a pup, and he'd been by my side for eighteen years. Flynn had followed me everywhere. Even if he was comfortably sleeping on the rug, he'd get up and follow if I moved from the living room to the kitchen. Not because he was needy—just so he could always be with me. He loved to be outside running around in the fresh air, trying to herd something, sniffing for a tasty treat in the feed buckets, and making friends with the horses. Wherever I sat, he'd be there at my feet. He loved curling up beside me in the evening, placing his warm head against my body, and falling peacefully asleep in my lap.

It frightened Jorge how heartbroken I became after losing Flynn. No matter what he said, I was inconsolable. Then one evening after dinner, he took my hand and said, "Come here, I want to show you something." He led me to the front yard by the pasture, to the spot where we'd buried Flynn. I didn't want to see it, that patch of dirt where the grass had not yet grown back. Instead, I focused on the big maple tree in the bloom of late spring and the birds singing in its branches. As we drew near, my heart skipped a beat, and I put a hand to my chest. There under the leafy canopy, Jorge had placed a beautiful cement bench, and around it he'd planted a soft border of lavender-hued bushes. I took a step back, taking it all in. On the bench, he'd set Flynn's bowl and empty collar. I blinked hard, but the tears welled.

"Go ahead, try it out," Jorge said.

I sat on the bench, closed my eyes, and tried to release the grief that blocked me from all the happy thoughts of my departed friend. When I opened my eyes again, the sun was setting in streaks of pink and orange. I felt as if something had broken open inside me and fluttered away against the fading sun. I motioned for Jorge to join me. He sat beside me, and I leaned into him. In our deepest, darkest struggles we are always stronger together, Jorge and me. I ran my hand across the smooth, cool surface of the loving gift Jorge had supplied when words couldn't heal. I could almost feel Flynn there with us, lying in the grass at our feet.

15

"Follow your heart."

We stepped off the airplane in Athens, Greece, into some of the most beautiful country I'd ever seen. As we traveled to the nearby port of Rafina, we were greeted by turquoise waters, miles of pristine beaches, and brilliant white houses ascending a hill. "I feel like I've just arrived in heaven," I said.

We were there after being contacted by a businesswoman named Mina. She had read about us on social media and begged us to bring some horses. "Can you help me start a Gentle Carousel here?" she'd asked repeatedly.

At first we weren't at all receptive to the idea. "I appreciate your interest," I answered, "but I just don't think it would work." How could we put our life's mission in someone else's hands? How could we trust that the horses would be safe, the people would be served, and Gentle Carousel would be run as lovingly as we ran it?

Mina was determined. "This is what our country needs," she said. "I want to bring something special to my people." The more she talked, the more I realized how deeply she cared about her country. She was smart, and not only did she have a good head on her shoulders but she also had experience and compassion. We began to take her pleas more seriously. "Is this the right thing to do?" I asked Jorge one night after hanging up from her phone call.

"I think," he said, "sometimes you have to follow your heart."

Mina didn't give up. She told us that she needed our assistance because she wanted quality miniature horses, which weren't available in Greece, and the benefit of our experience in training them. She respected our reputation and longed to become a part of Gentle Carousel. In addition, she needed our help convincing the city officials and businesses that miniature therapy horses could be valuable in her country. Eventually, she had us thinking that it was a possibility, so Jorge visited her in Greece to gather more information. Now I was thrilled for the chance to join him and check things out. This could be an amazing opportunity.

The spunky woman with long blond hair and infectious energy ran up to us. She wore loose white slacks and a flowing peach top. "*Yassas!*" she said in Greek. "Hello, welcome!" She hugged us warmly. I liked her instantly.

Mina first arranged to take us to the Lyreio Orphanage, where she hoped someday to bring miniature therapy horses. We drove up a long, winding driveway lined by a stone wall. The large, white stone building with rows of arched windows sat way up on a mountain overlooking the gorgeous hillside. I would never forget my first sight of this orphanage on that mountain—it was majestic and humble at the same time. There were beautiful patios and places to play outside. What we think of as the traditional orphanage no longer exists in the United States. But in Greece, thousands of children live in orphanages, in part due to Greece's devastating economic crisis. "The kids here range from babies to twenty-one years of age," Mina said. "Some spend their entire childhood here."

I followed her through an archway to the front door. The moment I walked inside, I felt welcome. The orphanage felt friendly. The rooms were bright and airy, with high ceilings and clean tile floors, smooth white walls, and huge windows. The dining room held rows of wooden tables with white tablecloths and vases of fresh cut flowers. Mina showed us to a long beige sofa in a living room, where I set down my box of books. We spoke for a while, and then two nuns dressed in long black robes and black headscarves escorted a group of youngsters inside. The boys wore white shirts and dark pants, and the girls wore dresses. They smiled and sang the sweetest song for us that they'd memorized in English. I wanted to reach out and hug every one of them.

"We have something for you," I said. I held up several bound photo books I'd made, each filled with pictures of the horses running and playing. The children's faces lit up, and they all clapped when I handed the books out. You'd think

I'd given them the newest toys or the finest chocolates in the world. I watched them gather into little groups and delight in the pictures. They were so happy with such a simple thing. This was someplace special.

Later, Jorge took out his iPad and showed the nuns videos of the horses. The nuns huddled together to view the screen and smiled and laughed. They were enthralled. I glanced over at Jorge, and we exchanged a knowing look. That was the moment when we both agreed we'd do whatever we could to make Gentle Carousel Greece a reality.

That afternoon we sat with Mina at a lovely bistro in town, eating grilled fish and pita with creamy tzatziki. Mina's organization and efficiency impressed us—she had everything planned. "I won't let you down," Mina said. "I promise." Not only did she plan to work with the orphanage, but she hoped to bring the horses to a children's hospital in Athens that is cutting-edge for cancer treatment.

"Mina, tell us, why are you so interested in doing this?" I asked.

She nodded sincerely. "I see what you do with Gentle Carousel. I want to bring that kind of love to the children of Greece."

After lunch, Mina brought us to her stables. "This is Billy," she said. The adorable, light-brown pony trotted up to me and pushed his nose against my arm. He had a shaggy mane and a thin white blaze down his face. He clearly loved Mina. "We found Billy in a teeny backyard in Athens. The grass was all overgrown, with weeds everywhere, and there was Billy standing there, nothing to do and nowhere to go. He was scrawny and dirty. He hadn't been groomed in many, many years. I found out later he was about ten years old. He had most likely been there for all ten years, just standing there. It broke my heart. I knocked on the door and spoke to the owners. Somehow, I convinced them to let me take him. In hindsight, it really wasn't too hard. I drove to the store and bought some carrots, then used the carrots to coax him into the back of my van. He just walked right in, weak as he was. He loved those carrots! When I got him home and gave him healthy food, fresh water, and lots of attention and room to run, I watched him transform from a lonely creature to one who is full of life and has lots of love to give."

I knew she had the right heart for the work. I felt deep down that Mina and her mission would be successful.

Setting up an organization outside of our own country, particularly one involving live animals, was beyond challenging. We chose three young horses we'd just started training, and bought two more. Jorge and I spent hours working with the airport and government to find a way to transport the horses to Greece. Finally, Jorge was able to fly to Miami and wait there while the horses were in quarantine, then continue the flight to Rafina with the horses he'd lovingly prepared for their new life.

Mina's establishment flourished like a lush oasis. She called it Magic Garden, named after our horse Magic. Behind an arched white stone gate spread immaculate grounds with

153

an exercise ring adorned with colorful pennants. I couldn't have imagined anything more perfect.

We always stay in touch on the phone, and we have returned to Greece many times. Mina has become a treasured friend. Once, we decided to take a few extra days and vacation on the gorgeous island of Santorini. Mina would be joining us. Before we left, Mina received a phone call from a man who said he knew of a little horse on the island that needed help. He told Mina, "She's been living in a pen on some land beside a local business since she was born. But they're selling the property, and now there's nowhere else for her to go."

I thought of Mina's pony Billy and his previous living conditions. None of us wanted to think what might happen to this little horse if we didn't help. We agreed to stop by.

When we arrived, the situation was worse than we'd imagined. The tiny, barren pen held only rocks and an old tire. The horse had been living there all alone in those conditions for eight years. We were told that sometimes tourists tossed her a few scraps of food—bread or crackers with little nutrition. There was an old bucket on the ground with a sign suggesting that visitors could tote water for her if they wanted. It was unclear how often anyone did.

The horse was filthy, and her hooves were a mess. "But she actually is a miniature horse," I said, surprised. We were expecting a bigger horse, or at least a pony like Billy. Miniature horses are not native to Santorini. We learned that years earlier, someone had brought one over and she'd had a foal. After the mare died, the little horse was left alone. We had to help, but we weren't set up for a rescue. We'd traveled by plane; we didn't even have a vehicle—we'd been brought over to see the horse by someone at the hotel. Still, looking at the poor creature, we knew we had to do something.

Mina has the biggest heart. She called one of her employees and asked him to bring the company van. This was not a simple task—Santorini is accessible by boat but would require a ten-hour ride each way.

When the company van arrived, we pushed down a section of the wire fence and Jorge stepped over. We learned that the horse's name was Giselle and that she'd never been out of her pen before. Yet she trusted Jorge as he gently slipped a halter over her head and led her away. I imagine she must have been thinking, *Just get me out of here. I don't care where I'm going; it's got to be better than this.* Although we had worried  that she might not want to go in the van, she walked right in.

In transporting a horse we didn't know, a lot could go wrong. Giselle might grow anxious on such a long ride and want to get out. But we'd bought some hay and food in the hopes it would keep her happy. Jorge rode with her in the back of the van, while Mina and I flew back to the port. I couldn't stop thinking about Giselle. She'd never done anything wrong and didn't deserve the hardships she'd been forced to endure. I was so relieved she'd have the best life waiting for her with Mina.

It was late at night by the time we all arrived back at Magic Garden. I'll never forget those first moments, opening the van

155

and watching Giselle get a look at her new home. Despite her difficult life, she was a sweet little horse and followed Jorge willingly. We put her in a stall by herself—we had to keep her quarantined until she checked out with the vet. When the other horses heard and sensed the new arrival, they whinnied. Giselle perked her ears and pranced in her stall and whinnied back. She looked so happy. She hadn't seen another horse almost her whole life, but she was so excited to be there around the others.

Giselle is now healthy and as loved as any horse ever could be. Her big, deep eyes are expressive and trusting. Giselle and Billy are best friends and work together at the education center, teaching children about humane treatment of animals. Gentle Carousel Greece is thriving. The horses have become celebrities in all of Greece. They've been on national television and are known throughout the country. They can go inside any store or business and are the only animals in Greece allowed inside a hospital. The horses are loved, and they do so much good.

In the summer of 2018, however, seven years after Gentle Carousel Greece opened, we received word that wildfires had swept through Rafina, destroying much of the village and claiming more than a hundred lives. After receiving the news, Jorge and I stood outside our barn, thinking of our friends so far away. "I can't believe it. Is everyone safe? Are the horses okay?"

"Mina is safe. All the horses are safe," Jorge told me. I let out a sigh of relief. "But the fires traveled so fast, it was devastating. Mina and the volunteers reacted immediately, loading the horses into vans, but the roads got so clogged they had to get out and abandon the vehicles. The horses had to run with their handlers all the way to the sea, dodging cars and flames down to the shore. But they made it."

On the beach, terrified people had jumped into the Aegean Sea. "The horses remained calm," Mina had told Jorge. "They were amazing. Once they reached safety on the shore, people came up to them seeking comfort. Everyone was scared. Young ones were terrified. But the horses helped."

I asked about the beautiful orphanage that we'd visited on our first trip to Greece. "The nuns got everyone out of the orphanage safely," Mina said. "The children all escaped. But the orphanage is destroyed." While I was devastated at the loss of the physical building, I knew that the loving spirit of Lyreio Orphanage would stay alive.

"And what about Magic Garden? Jorge asked.

"That is something most amazing," Mina said. "The fires were all around us. The firefighters worked hard to protect us. I am so grateful. They stopped the fires just before reaching Magic Garden. There was a car on fire right outside the gates—it's still there, melted. The flames went right up to our door. Everything is burned all around us. But Magic Garden survived."

We were in awe of the miraculous outcome. We asked what we could do to help. In the following weeks, we gathered supplies and traveled to Greece to bring aid. There had been eighty fatalities in Rafina. Rebuilding the community would take months. But I believed in the strength of the people I'd met there.

Sometime later, we heard from Mina. "We're working to teach young people about fire safety," she said. "And we have a new representative, an ambassador who will go into the schools to help reach the children. Sort of like your Smokey the Bear."

"That's wonderful, Mina," I said. "Who is this new ambassador?"

Mina's voice was filled with pride. "There was once a little horse who was saved and will now help save others," she said. "The new ambassador is Giselle."

16

"Everyone can make a difference."

Colorful fabrics formed tall stacks atop long tables. Tangles of yarn, clouds of cottony filling, and rows of sewing machines lined the room. Dozens of workers sat busily cutting fabric, sewing, and stuffing toy horses. It looked like Santa's workshop.

"They're going to be surprised," I whispered to Jorge, standing in the doorway with Magic by our side.

The men and women of The Villages active adult retirement community diligently volunteer making the little stuffed horses that Gentle Carousel distributes. Several times a year, they pack hundreds of the plush toys in clear plastic bags and deliver them to the farm so that Jorge and I can give them to children.

The project began with a simple observation—a woman who volunteered with us when we visited hospitals noticed the little plush horses we gave each child. *What a lovely gesture*, she thought. A gesture, she knew, that was an added

expense for the organization. So she made a trip to the dollar store and bought a whole bag full of plush horses to donate. Whenever she found a good deal somewhere, she stocked up.

Another Gentle Carousel volunteer, Marcy, took the idea a step further. She had a connection with an organization called Operation Shoebox, whose mission is to make care packages for service members and children in need. Marcy thought that sewing plush horses for Gentle Carousel would fit the organization's mission and would be a perfect project for residents at The Villages. So she made the arrangements, using a horse pattern designed by a pediatric nurse so it would be safe for children of all ages. The volunteers work diligently, and every year they produce enough soft horses for Gentle Carousel to hand out at all our events. Even most of the older adults like receiving the plush horses. I am in awe at how one small but important need has been so generously supplied by dozens of caring individuals, most of whom we never even meet. That is why our surprise stop at The Villages that day meant

160

so much. I wanted the volunteers to know we appreciated all their work.

We walked into the facility, Magic leading the way. All the stitchers looked up, and then, recognizing the horse, dropped what they were doing and came over to meet us.

"Magic, it's you!" A woman bent down and pushed the pretty floral-patterned toy horse she'd been working on in front of Magic's big blue eyes.

"Come, take a tour," a gentleman said. He proudly showed us the stations where the horse shapes emerged beneath the pattern and where yarn was transformed into manes and tails. Nearly every person wanted to show Magic the plush horse they were constructing. "Your creativity is amazing," I said. "I love the combinations of colors and designs."

"But you do the real work," a woman with a long braid and rosy cheeks said.

I spread my arms as if to embrace them all. "We all help, all in our own ways. Me, I couldn't sew a stitch. It takes all of us. We're so very grateful. And we have something we want to show you."

Jorge set up a video, and the whole group watched a little boy in a wheelchair holding his stuffed horse, a little girl hooked up to IVs showing her horse to a doctor, boys and girls hugging their horses and smiling. "We wanted you to see who is being blessed by your work," Jorge said. "Your kindness and generosity provide so many people with a tangible way to remember the visit."

The woman with the braid spoke again. "And now, after Magic's visit to us here today, we'll always remember why we're doing this."

Looking around, I was overwhelmed by the people who pitched in. It wasn't easy for me to accept help from others. I was the one to take charge, to step in when needed. I'd always been that way. When I was young, I was the kid taking home the injured chipmunk, the bird with a broken wing, and the abandoned kitten in the alley.

One time I was walking home from school when I came upon a beagle puppy with deep, sad eyes. He was huddled in a tight ball inside a cardboard box that had been dumped at the curb. As I watched him trembling, waiting for his owners to come back for him, I couldn't keep walking. I knew the family had moved away. In my neighborhood, people came and went. Most were good pet parents, but there were times a pet got left behind. I scooped up the puppy and cradled him in my arms. He didn't even squirm as I snuck him into a safe place in our backyard and made him a comfortable bed. When my parents weren't looking, I snuck him scraps of food. I cared for him like he was my own, even though my parents would never let me keep him.

After posting dozens of signs, one day I found the puppy a good home. It felt great, but all too soon it happened again. I'd find puppies, old dogs, kittens—all abandoned. And I took them all home. I even enlisted the help of a friend, and when our backyards filled up, we asked neighbors to let us use their yards. We built pens for the cats and used our babysitting money to buy food. At times I had more than I could handle. Of course, I wanted to keep them all. But I made hand-printed signs that I posted on telephone poles, and ran free classified ads in the newspaper in order to find them homes. I saved dozens of abandoned animals. Looking back, I realize that at the age of twelve I was running my own rescue organization.

I don't know what my parents thought of it all, but they never stopped me. My early independence shaped my desire to always be in control. Which is why whenever someone would approach me and ask, "How can I help?" my first instinct was always to say, "I've got this." But over time I've learned to accept these offers. I know how good it feels to help others, and quite frankly Gentle Carousel needs the help. Our events often attract a great deal of attention. Libraries and schools sometimes bring in more than a hundred children for events. The horses are not asked to work every day—we rotate them so that they get rest days between events. We receive more requests for visits than we can fill. So many people seem to be looking for the kind of care we provide.

"I want to help, but I don't know anything about horses," a young woman once told me after meeting us at a hospital. It was affirming to keep finding people who wanted to give of themselves to help others. All our needs ran through my mind—finalizing appointments, controlling crowds, organizing lines of children, handing out materials, turning on music and videos, keeping little hands and toes out of the way, answering parents' questions, coordinating with doctors and nurses, and protecting the horses from any mishaps. We could always use drivers . . . artists . . . musicians. One woman sewed beautiful decorative blankets for the horses and sometimes made clever costumes they could wear on

163

holidays to delight the children. A tech-savvy young man offered to help set up audiovisual equipment. Other volunteers would form a perimeter around the horses to keep them safe as we walked into crowded buildings. One volunteer told me that he loved watching the people's faces the mo-

ment they saw the mini horses, and he felt proud to know he was doing something to help.

Folks have many different talents, and so I welcomed with open arms that young woman who said she knew nothing about horses. "It doesn't matter that you've never worked with horses. There are many ways to volunteer," I said. "Everyone can make a difference." And that's often what people are craving: a way to make a difference. Accepting help is not a weakness. It is a way of letting others experience the blessing of helping.

We are grateful for all our many volunteers. Once we were at a popular equestrian event with tiny little Mercury, who was less than a year old. We got a call about a media event in another part of the vast facilities, and were asked if we could make it there in time. Mercury loved running, but I wasn't so sure my legs were willing to carry me up the steep hill and all the way to where the event was being held! So, Ellen and Steve, our volunteers that day, offered their shiny new white Mercedes convertible. Jorge and Mercury climbed in, and Steve drove them to the event in plenty of time. They saved the day! I had to laugh, because not everyone would plunk a horse in their brand-new luxury vehicle to help us out. That's the kind of caring volunteers and friends they are.

I met Claudia, another dear volunteer, when she offered to help us out at hospitals. While Jorge and I take the children to walk the horses down the pediatric corridors, Claudia hangs back with the parents. That's something I can rarely do because Jorge and I are keeping our focus on the horses and their interaction with the patients. But when I see the worry etched on the parents' faces, I'm always glad Claudia is there.

I often hear a mother or father confiding their worries about cancer, immune systems, and diseases that have taken a terrible toll on their lives. They wonder if their child will get better. As a retired nurse, Claudia is always willing to listen to anxious family members. "I understand," she says, and then the two will engage in a deep conversation, one that the parent needs and one that Claudia is uniquely equipped to provide.

After her first time volunteering, Claudia approached me, her face bright and smiling. "I'm so grateful for this opportunity," she said. "Now I can give the parents all the attention I wished I had time for when I was on duty."

"We're so happy you're here too," I told her.

Some of our volunteers are moved to help us after we've served them. For instance, a person who was helped by one of our horses during physical therapy may be able to give perspective to struggling patients in similar circumstances. A cancer survivor may offer a patient or loved one the hope they need to face the ordeals ahead.

Thoughts of all these faithful volunteers played across my mind as I helped Jorge load Magic into the trailer and we prepared to leave The Villages. We climbed into the truck and pulled away, carrying with us a new supply of plush horses and a fresh appreciation for every one of those amazing volunteers who gave their time to sew in order to make children happy.

I feel a deep appreciation for all the people who are dedicated to our mission—all the volunteers who make our work possible. We aren't alone. We are surrounded by others with strength and muscle, experience and wisdom, willing hearts and able hands. People want to help—good people whom we find everywhere we visit.

17

"All we wanted were the ponies."

As I watched Jorge's expression, I knew the news was bad. He hung up the phone. "There's been a shooting," he said.

I could never get used to hearing those words. "Oh no," I gasped. "Where?"

"Pulse nightclub in Orlando. Forty-nine dead. Fifty-three injured. What a nightmare."

We both sat in silence, trying to take it in. The next day we were asked to help. We brought three horses and visited with the families and friends of those who had been killed and the survivors struggling to deal with sights they could never unsee. One young woman approached the horses silently,

167

unable to verbalize her emotions. I whispered a prayer that the horses would soothe and comfort that woman, that although nothing could reverse the tragic incident, the connection with the horses would help her find a moment of peace. Others who had been there that night told the horses their shattering stories.

"I lost my best friend."

"He shot my partner."

"I narrowly escaped."

Husbands, fathers, sons and daughters—my heart broke at every poignant story.

The last day we were there, we went to the fire stations and police stations to check in on the first responders. They're a pretty tough lot in a crisis, getting the job done, so they're sometimes overlooked. "I try to keep my composure," one EMT said, pushing his hands deep in his pockets. "I was just doing my job." But he clung to Magic's neck as tightly as anyone else.

Before we left, we stopped to pay our respects at the make-shift memorial that had sprung up outside the nightclub, a graphite-gray one-story building with a wide awning out front. We walked Anthem up to the sidewalk beneath the tall Pulse nightclub sign. The ground around it was strewn with a mountain of sunflowers, long-stemmed roses, and Mylar balloons of every shape and color. The chain-link fence that surrounded the building was covered with banners, flags, paper chains, and posters with hearts and rainbows. Teddy bears, framed portraits, and wreaths leaned against the base. A sign hung across the chain links with the words "LOVE is greater than HATE" spelled out in colorful letters. Love. Always, even amid the trauma, we saw love.

Jorge and I stood quietly, and soon men and women, young and old, approached and asked Anthem for a hug. The little horse attended to each one, looking into their eyes, leaning into their hearts.

Later, we attended a press event, which included President Obama and local politicians. As we waited, two men in dark suits and sunglasses approached.

"Everyone has to move back," one of the men said.

We gathered everything and moved the horses across the street. As soon as we were settled, the Secret Service personnel came again and told us that we weren't far enough away. I looked around. Just how far away did they expect us to go? The sidewalks were full. We squeezed down the street as best we could.

"I hope we can still be of use," I sighed.

"The people who need us will find us," Jorge said.

And they did.

The press event ended, and the politicians made their way back to their vehicles. Reporters called in updates on their cell phones. Jorge and I noticed one woman breaking down her television equipment, removing a camera from its tripod. She gazed over at the nightclub, pain in her eyes. Although we always try to reach anyone who might be hurting, I hadn't before thought about the media. They have to ask tough questions and report with calm control, but when the microphones and cameras are off, they too have to grapple with the difficult events.

Jorge caught the woman's eye. "Do you want to visit with the horse?" he asked. She dropped her camera and ran over. "Yes!" she said, bending down and throwing her arms around Magic.

After the camera operator left, another woman approached, her expression just as anxious and hurt. "I'm a grief counselor," she told us, kneeling down to Magic and giving her a hug. And there we discovered another group of people the horses could reach out to—those who work to help others process grief yet who also need comfort to deal with deep feelings of their own.

We saw several children wandering about the memorial as well. I carried a bag with some of the plush horses that we regularly hand out at hospitals. When I saw a young girl with her family, I asked if she'd like to visit with Magic, and then I gave her a plush horse so that she could hold it and hug it and find some comfort in it. The girl thanked us and squeezed the horse tight to her chest. Then she ran off and placed it beside a pile of flowers at the memorial. I teared up at her sweet, surprising gesture.

Then another child appeared before me, looking at my bag hopefully. I smiled and gave him a plush horse, and he took the horse over and placed it on the memorial as well. The next thing I knew, all the children around me were standing in line, awaiting their own plush horse, which they then added to the piles of flowers and signs in front of the nightclub until my bag was empty. It was not how I had expected these horses would be used. I expected they would be hugged and cuddled by those in need of comfort. But this act of having something to place on the memorial comforted the children in just the way they needed.

After that, we returned to the van and made the trip home. We'd just gotten the horses settled when I received a phone call from someone in the Orange County offices. "We heard you were in town," she said. "We were wondering if you'd mind visiting the medical examiner's office."

"Actually, I'm sorry, we just got back home," I said.

"Oh. Umm, well . . . is there any chance you'd be coming back?" We always visited the first responders, the police, and medical professionals, but we had never visited the medical examiner's offices before. The caller explained how demanding and exhausting their job had been and how diligently they worked in the recovery, identification, and reunification process. "They were identifying victims and performing autopsies as quickly as possible to get the bodies back with the families." She added, "One of the doctors told me about the noise he couldn't get out of his head. It's the sound of cell phones ringing. You see, when they entered the building that night, phones were going off on the bodies of all the victims. It was friends and loved ones calling to see if they were okay."

Just as we had discovered at the memorial, there are countless groups of people who work hard behind the scenes during disasters and tragedies. The caller asked again if we might be able to return. "We just want to do something positive for them. I know most of them are animal lovers. Do you know what I heard one of them say? He said, 'We got the politicians . . . but all we wanted were the ponies.'"

The next day Jorge and I, three horses, and two volunteers made the trip back to Orlando. We entered the offices and walked Magic, Sweetheart, and Anthem down the halls, which were lined with men and women in business attire, white lab coats, or scrubs. Many of the workers pulled out their cell phones and took pictures; others got down on the floor to be closer to our little horses. A tall man in a blue oxford shirt introduced himself as Dr. Joshua Stephany, the chief medical examiner. "This is Anthem," Jorge said. "Would you like to show him around?"

The man's face lit up. Jorge handed over the lead and Dr. Stephany walked the little white horse with brown patches up and down the halls. He peeked into all the rooms with a big grin on his face, and the entire building seemed to glow with a genuine peacefulness.

We took our time and visited with as many people as we could. One woman hugged Sweetheart and took selfies with her. A man with glasses sat solemnly on the floor in the hall, his emotions taking over. Anthem sensed his mood and walked over to lay his head on the man's shoulder. "You guys seeing this?" the man said, his voice wavering.

Jorge and I hadn't asked Anthem to do this. Sometimes the horses just know.

18

"You bring books to life."

The big outdoor literacy festival at O'Leno State Park in High Springs, Florida, was one of the highlights of my year. We'd already been on the road for a whole week, however, and while the horses were well-rested, I hadn't had a break. I leaned over and whispered to Jorge, "I'm sorry to say this, but I'm exhausted. Do you think it would be okay to get out of here as soon as this is over?"

Moonshadow stood beside Jorge and me under the pavilion, where we would share a story with the kids. I love anything and everything to do with books . . . always have, ever since I was a little girl. When I was young, I must have read every horse book in the library: *Misty of Chincoteague*,

The Red Pony, Black Beauty, National Velvet. I dreamed that those horses were my best friends. Sometimes, when my family had just moved and I hadn't met any girls my age, the fictional horses were the closest thing I had to a best friend. Later, when I became a teacher, it was my goal to help every student develop a love of reading. But not every child did. Some struggled to sound out the words, some had trouble grasping the meaning, and some were never exposed to books at home. In the low-income neighborhood where I once taught, many families couldn't afford books and never spent time in a library. I wanted to find a way to connect those children with books.

When we started working with miniature horses, I saw a way. I'd already been bringing animals to my classroom. Students who did their work were rewarded by getting to spend time with the animals. But the animals provided much more than just academic motivation. Feeding the goldfish helped teach responsibility. Holding a gerbil taught lessons in compassion. And even the most disruptive students relaxed when stroking the soft fur of an angora rabbit. From those experiences, I knew that horses could teach the children as well, and I hoped they could teach them about books.

I became even more excited about the opportunity when I realized that one of our horses looks very much like the horse on the cover of Marguerite Henry's book *Misty of Chincoteague.* The storybook Misty is mostly white and has a brown patch over one eye. When I first saw our Misty, it was as if she'd stepped right off the cover of the book. That was how I felt when I read stories as a child—that the characters were coming out to play with me. What if other children could feel that way too? What if they could learn

174

to love books by interacting with beloved characters in the form of our horses? So we held an event at the library where I read a chapter from Marguerite Henry's book. The children listened to the story. Then Jorge walked into the room with the little horse.

"It's Misty!" the boys and girls gasped. I was thrilled that they made the connection. All of a sudden, the youngsters became engaged and enthusiastic, chattering together and shooting their hands up to ask questions about the horse and the book. This was just what I'd been hoping for. Many of the children also left with brand-new library cards.

The librarian beamed. "You bring books to life!"

That's why we always carry books with us wherever we go—thousands of them—and why we bring the horses to schools and libraries. I love the children's enthusiasm and their eager questions when I read to them.

"How old is she?" one of the children will always ask when they meet a horse.

"She's five years old. How old are you?" I might answer.

"I'm five too!" the child might say, which leads to a discussion of the similarities and differences between five-year-old kids and five-year-old horses.

Sweetheart, one of our all-white horses, looks like a magical unicorn, especially when we add sparkles in her mane and a costume horn. So when she visits libraries, we read books about unicorns. Magic sometimes helps us portray Black Beauty. And even Bart, our sweet miniature donkey, gets to shine—he looks just like the donkey on the cover of *Brighty of the Grand Canyon* by Marguerite Henry. The children love seeing Brighty in person! Sometimes we read Winnie the Pooh books and bring Bart to play Eeyore. We play the song "The House on Pooh Corner" as Jorge leads him in. Nearly every child knows all about sad ol' Eeyore, and they ask him questions: "How is Tigger?" "Do you know Roo?" "Do you really eat thistles?"

Sometimes we teach lessons about kindness. One morning we walked into a classroom with Circus, our white horse covered with black polka dots. Everyone enjoys seeing a spotted horse. I read them

Eric Carle's book *The Artist Who Painted a Blue Horse*. Then I read an extra-large picture book that I created about a horse who got a different-colored spot every time he did something kind. I always tie in this story with an activity to help reinforce the message. "Can anyone tell me about something kind you did today?" I asked.

A girl in the front raised her hand. "I shared my lunch with Sebastian because he forgot his."

"That's a very thoughtful thing to do," I said. "Now you may come up here and paint a spot on Circus." I handed her a small jar of safe, nontoxic "paint"—which is really just shampoo with a little color added. She carefully dipped her finger into the jar and dabbed the paint onto Circus's side.

Seeing this and wanting to paint the horse themselves, everyone's hands shot up.

"I hugged my dog this morning."

"I helped the teacher hand out papers."

"I let Myra go first in line even though it was my turn."

The goal was for every child to paint a fingerprint-sized spot on Circus so they could all recognize how good it felt to be kind. When we got to the last little boy, I asked him if he could think of something kind he'd done that day.

After some thought, he looked at me, shrugged, and said, "I got nothing."

I stifled a laugh as I guided him toward an answer. "Well, you waited there very patiently for your turn, didn't you? That was kind."

"Yeah, I guess it was!" he said with a smile, then went up and painted his spot on Circus.

When we were done, Circus was covered in all different colors, just like the horse in my storybook. "Isn't Circus beautiful? See how much all your little acts of kindness add up?" I said. "Circus hopes you'll always remember to be kind."

The children nodded and agreed. We gathered all around Circus and took a group picture. And back at home, Circus got a nice bath.

Many children have had some experience with dogs, but most haven't been up close with a horse. Our miniature horses are small, but they are still bigger than most dogs. Some children who are afraid of big dogs feel a little anxious when we come to their class. One time we went to a preschool for our literacy presentation. Before leaving, we gave every child the opportunity to pat or hug the horses. Everyone took a turn saying hello to Magic except for one little girl. I wanted her to have the chance to interact, to have no regrets once she got home. When I was reading the story, I'd noticed that she was enamored with her hair. The children had nap time before we arrived, and she must have felt her hair wasn't just right. She kept fussing with the strands and tossing her head. So I went up to her and gently said, "You don't have to hug Magic if you don't want. But would you like to fix her hair?" I handed the little girl the sparkly pink brush from my tote bag. Her eyes grew wide and she accepted the brush, then very carefully laid it against Magic's forelock.

"That's right," I said. "Like this." I showed her how to brush the mane. "Good job! She looks beautiful now." The girl lit right up and was so proud of her work. She left having had a positive interaction with an animal instead of a fearful encounter.

One boy with special needs was mesmerized by Magic, patting her face and speaking to her in his own special way. His mother watched in awe. "This is the first time he's ever interacted with an animal," she said. Magic has a way of putting people at ease.

I think all the children have fun when we dress the horses in fanciful outfits. One time we were doing an elaborate production of *Fritz and the Beautiful Horses* by Jan Brett. Fritz the pony is excluded from a group of beautiful horses but later becomes a hero when he rescues the local children. I love this book because it teaches that size and appearance don't matter and that anyone can make a big impact. Rainbow played the part of Fritz because he is so small. The library was packed with boys and girls, and we enlisted extra volunteers to help. The children were so excited, and I didn't want to let them down, so I put a lot of effort into making this event extravagant.

Part of the fun was that the children themselves got to play some of the characters from the book. We gave them beautiful dresses and capes to wear. In addition, a volunteer had sewn elegant costumes for the horses. The skit involved several costume changes, so I put the extra outfits on a folding table out on the front lawn. The plan was to take the horses outside for a quick costume change between scenes. Everything was going well until I rushed outside to scoop up the next outfit. There at my folding table was a flock of ladies rummaging through the piles of clothing and chattering loudly as they examined the sparkly costumes. I approached with a smile on my face, but inside I was wondering why on earth they would be going through our stuff.

One woman with a bulky pocketbook slung over one shoulder and several of the costumes draped over her arm barely looked up as she asked, "How much?"

"For what?" I said.

"How much for these scarves and capes?" she asked.

"I'll give you five dollars for this," another lady chimed in, holding up a blue horse blanket embroidered with sequins.

I stifled a laugh. The ladies thought it was a library yard sale! I got the costumes back, and fortunately the rest of the show went off without a hitch. At the end of the story, Rainbow donned the dazzling blue blanket. All the children gathered around and hugged him, just like Fritz in the book. It was beautiful and worth every bit of effort.

These are the types of events that mean so much to me. That's why we are eager to participate in them—particularly the literacy festival at O'Leno State Park that day. Even as exhausted as I felt, it was important to me. When it was our turn, I read a story while Jorge led little Moonshadow around the stage. As she pranced along, I watched the children's faces light up. It felt good that they were experiencing literature in a fun and positive way. I hoped it would remain with them all their years.

"Okay," Jorge said, steering me away from the stage. "Let's get going, like you said." I gathered our supplies and,

thinking of the cool air-conditioning in the van, started to make my way out of the park. It would feel good to put my feet up for a few minutes.

We'd just separated from the thick of the crowd when I saw a mom and her young daughter resting under a tree. The little girl wore purple sneakers and flowered leg braces with thick pink Velcro straps. She looked at Moonshadow, then did a double take, her eyes wide. The mom seemed almost as excited as the girl. I slowed down.

"But . . ." Jorge said. "You wanted to . . ."

I stopped.

"Hello!" I said to the girl. "Would you like to say hi to my friend? Her name is Moonshadow. What's yours?"

"Paris," the little girl said, flashing the most beautiful smile. Jorge looked at me, his eyebrows raised—*I thought you wanted to get right home?*—but led Moonshadow over. Moonshadow walked right up to the little girl and looked into her eyes, and Paris glowed with delight. Moonshadow nuzzled under Paris's chin—she liked her. Paris reached up—her movements slow and deliberate—and kissed Moonshadow's nose.

180

"This is the first time I ever touched a horse!" Paris said.

"Oh wow! You're a natural!"

Although I was tired and ready to unwind, Moonshadow was in no hurry. She hung beside Paris, not wanting to leave, as if she sensed something special. I looked at the little girl, and something about her urged me on too.

"Paris, would you like to help us walk our horse?" Glancing at her leg braces, I wasn't sure how well she could walk, but the horses had assisted many patients in physical therapy and rehab hospitals before, so I felt it would be okay. And Paris looked like she had spunk. She nodded vigorously, and her mom agreed.

Although getting around was clearly a challenge for this child, I marveled at how she so willingly accepted. Jorge hooked up the double lead line and Paris got to her feet. I gave Paris the line and she took the first few cautious steps, following Moonshadow along the path. Jorge led them around a short course and circled back. Her cheeks glowed rosy as she lowered herself to the ground. "Today was the first time I ever walked a horse!" she said, grinning. Then she added, "And on my birthday too!"

"Today's your birthday?" I asked.

"Yes! I'm six today!" she said, holding up six fingers. Jorge and I wished her a happy birthday, and Moonshadow gave her an extra nuzzle.

As we left, I felt a warm glow in my own cheeks, and it wasn't from the heat and fatigue. It was because Moonshadow had taken a special interest in Paris. The extra time and effort involved weren't part of my plan on an already exhausting day. But Moonshadow knew it was exactly what one little girl needed on her sixth birthday.

19

"Don't forget to have fun."

After any event, we not only let the horses shake it off but we also give them several days off to rest, run in the pasture, relax, and play. "Don't forget to have fun," I always say as I watch them trot off and join their friends.

It's not easy, but I also try to heed those words in order to keep things in balance. Life is meant to be experienced and also enjoyed. So we schedule in some lighter activities to provide a break from the more demanding ones.

One summer we were invited to spend a day at Zoo Atlanta to help administrators determine if the facility was in compliance with the Americans with Disabilities Act.

They wanted to know how accessible the grounds were for service animals. Although we were doing something important, we were still having fun. As we walked around, we were followed by a huge entourage—a guide, a PR person, a veterinarian, zookeepers, and a videographer. Because there was so much ground to cover—they wanted us to traverse the entire zoo—Magic toured half and Sweetheart did the other half.

We were escorted over bridges and into shops and restaurants by the zoo staff. At the habitats, we were amazed to see how the horses interacted with other species. Magic was interested in all the animals she saw, but she was most interested in a raccoon-sized Asian mammal called a tanuki, which I think looks a little like a wolverine. When a tanuki came up and put its paws on the glass, Magic got really close and the two checked each other out. "She's never seen an animal like that before," I said. Neither had I.

Later, we walked Sweetheart past the tiger exhibit. The tigers looked less comfortable with the presence of a horse than the tanuki had. They eyed Sweetheart, then one of the tigers ran up and hit the glass. I quickly moved on, but Sweetheart didn't flinch. She just watched curiously. She had been trained to remain calm in unusual situations—even a tiger charging.

I was most excited to see the twin baby pandas that had just been born. They spent a lot of time eating, but they did pause to exchange glances with us.

On the way out, we passed an elephant in its jungle habitat. As we walked over a little footbridge, the elephant spotted us, raised its trunk, and trumpeted. Sweetheart paused and whinnied back. The elephant trumpeted again. I listened, fascinated, as the two of them went back and forth, conversing in their own ways. I wish I knew what they were saying. When we were done, the staff was pleased that the zoo had been accessible for a well-trained miniature horse. And Jorge and I left with a new appreciation for less-familiar animals, as well as a fascination at the way different species interact and even communicate with each other.

Another regular visit we always enjoy is to O'Leno State Park. Scout has been going there ever since he was a foal and was even named a Junior Park Ranger. As Jorge walked him out of the trailer one day, Scout was frisky and lively. "He knows we're here," Jorge said.

Scout loves running on the nature trails and meeting friends in the education center. I buckled him into his green blanket with the state park patch on it. At certain times of the year, the park accepts gently used books instead of the regular admission price. By the end of the day the collection box would be full, and we would then bring Scout to at-risk neighborhoods to deliver the books.

We set out on the park's hiking trails. Scout had been there so many times, he knew his way and where he wanted to go. Hikers stopped and chatted with us, and Scout stood patiently and gave everyone a friendly nuzzle, but I could tell he wanted to keep going. A short way down the path, we came upon a boy who was about ten years old. Scout stopped for a moment. The boy was standing with his back to a long suspension bridge, and he had his head down and his arms crossed. The boy's father and sister were up ahead on the bridge, trying to get him to cross. He remained firm.

This bridge is beautiful and one of the park's highlights, but not everyone finds it comfortable to cross. It's long and narrow and hangs high above a river that cuts through the woods. There are wire safety barriers on either side, but some people find it disconcerting to see all the way down. And when you walk across, you may feel unsteady. There are those who embrace the wobble and run and jump and bounce their way across the bridge. But anyone who is even a little uncomfortable with heights might have trouble.

Scout watched the child and then took the path that led right to him. The boy smiled as we approached, then got down on his knees and patted Scout's neck and mane and laughed. I saw the positive effect Scout had on him and thought we could help. "Do you think you might like to walk across with Scout?" I asked.

Crossing a suspended bridge is not an easy task for a horse. For one thing, a horse's depth of field is far narrower than a human's. The uncertainty of a bridge's movement beneath their hooves also presents particular challenges. We're always careful to introduce new situations gradually. Every new surface takes getting used to, and Jorge had been working on this particular bridge with Scout.

The boy looked up curiously, but I could tell he was still unsure. "You see, Scout's just learning to walk on this bridge, and he could use a little help." This was true. Scout and Jorge had practiced, but we'd only crossed it once before. But maybe the boy would give it a try if he thought he was helping Scout.

186

With his family's encouragement, the boy agreed. We set him up with the double lead line and we all started across together. Scout kept up the pace, staying between Jorge and the boy. It was amazing, really, for a horse to accomplish this. He had to trust us. The young boy was so focused on Scout, he didn't even think about the unsteady bridge or look down over the rails at the drop below. When we all reached the other side, the boy cheered and hugged Scout. "You did it!" he told Scout.

"*You* did it!" I told him. Later, he told me that the bridge was now his favorite part of the trail.

When we were done, we gathered the donated books and later delivered them to a homeless shelter. One young girl was especially excited to see the box of books we delivered. "You must be a good reader," I said.

"I am!" she said. "I already know ten words!" Then she looked at Scout. "How many words does he know?" I thought it was such a clever question.

"Not as many as you!" Jorge answered. The little girl beamed with pride.

Another fun—and exciting—experience was getting to work with a real movie star: Burt Reynolds. Castille Landon, a Florida-based actress, writer, and director, contacted us because she'd been searching for a baby miniature horse to appear in her movie. A movie? Alongside Burt Reynolds? Count us in!

The film, *Apple of my Eye*, is about a young girl who becomes blind after a tragic horseback riding accident and then uses a miniature horse as her guide animal. They already had a horse actor for the main role but needed a baby horse for a couple of the scenes. At the time, Anthem was just the right age. We drove him, along with his big, inflatable soccer ball, Wilson, down to the Southeastern Guide Dogs facility outside of Tampa, where they were shooting the film.

When we first arrived on the set, a vet checked Anthem thoroughly to make sure he was healthy. We did a lot of standing around that day. We learned something about how movies are made—they do take after take after take. Anthem played outside and took naps in the trailer while we waited. When it was time for his scenes, Jorge and I watched from behind the cameras.

In his first scene, a young actress sat with Anthem's head on her lap. She was so taken with him, and I liked the way she stroked his nose tenderly. The older horse, Apple, was at her other side. Burt Reynolds stood nearby, leaning on a cane. Anthem was supposed to be just-born, and he lay there peacefully and even closed his eyes. He seemed to enjoy the patting. "I think he's asleep," I whispered to Jorge. They did the scene six or seven times. Afterward, Burt Reynolds came up to us and graciously told us that Anthem was the cutest little horse he'd ever seen. I knew he had horses of his own. "Thank you. Coming from you, that's a real compliment," I said.

The other scene was a Christmas scene, with the family posing for a photo around a beautifully decorated tree. Anthem stood with the young actress and looked around curiously. And that was a wrap! His acting day was over. We felt like proud parents.

Whether the horses are helping a patient, appearing before a crowd of people, or making a movie, we are proud of them. Our mission is to help and comfort people during difficult times. When we can add something to make them smile or laugh, it's a true bonus.

20

"There's a pony on the phone."

Conventioneers at the massive Javits Center in New York City would ordinarily be able to approach our horses, rub their necks, and give them a big hug, but not that February of 2020. Organizers had initiated new policies limiting contact and recommending that as much as possible people avoid touching each other, shaking hands, or patting the horses. In a place where thousands of people were gathering together to discuss and examine new products, this would be a challenge.

When we agreed to attend the huge international toy fair, we had heard news reports about the new coronavirus in

189

other countries. By the time we arrived in the Big Apple, a few cases were being reported in the United States, but experts believed the risk of infection was low. The convention would still be held. Nevertheless, in such a crowded area, we were advised to take a few precautions, so restrictions were put in place to keep people from getting too close to each other and to the horses.

The exposition was packed with toy manufacturers presenting exciting new product trends to retailers. We had been asked to bring two miniature horses to help showcase a display for Spirit, a popular children's book and television character. We generally don't participate in strictly commercial ventures, but when we realized that the all-expenses-paid trip would enable us to visit many hospitals along the way, we agreed. Magic, being the most experienced, and Moonshadow made the trip with us. They didn't look anything like Spirit, the buckskin wild mustang stallion in the book and movie illustrations, but they would be there as Spirit's friends.

It took a village—okay, more like a metropolis—to help us undertake such a venture with two miniature horses in New York. A farm outside of the city provided lodging for us and the horses, plus exercise rings where they could run and play. Police cordoned off a parking spot right outside the convention center and stood guard around our spacious horse van equipped with box stalls big enough that the horses could lie down if they desired. Organizers guided us to our setup location and made sure we had everything we needed. Our hosts provided us with adorable white blankets with blue trim and the Spirit logo emblazoned on the sides, and they created a fabulous display with artificial turf, rail fencing, barn doors, a giant cardboard cutout of the fictional Palomino Bluffs Riding Academy, and a bench where people could sit and pose for pictures near the horses. One volunteer from Florida accompanied us, and we had two additional volunteers from New York who walked the horses back and forth to the van for breaks and made sure they had water as well as rest time and play time.

We always strive to help others whenever we have the horses out, so we were thrilled that an organization arranged for critically ill children to come through first and experience a room filled with the newest, brightest, and most exciting toys in the world! Magic seemed to relate in a special way to these children and loved making friends with them. Throughout the weekend more than thirty thousand toy vendors and businesspeople attended from all over the world, and many stopped by to meet the horses and pose for pictures.

There wasn't much time to explore the bustling city, but we did stroll a few blocks past the hot dog stands and yellow cabs. Magic and Moonshadow did great amid the crowds and traffic. They say that not much fazes New Yorkers, but some pedestrians did a double take at seeing miniature horses walking down the crowded sidewalk.

When we returned to our parking spot, the police officer guarding the van grinned sheepishly. "Er, could I just do a quick FaceTime with you guys and my kids?" he asked. We smiled as he punched in the number. "Kids! You'll never guess who Daddy is guarding today!" He turned the phone to show them the horses. I could see his children's excited faces and hear their happy shrieks as they watched their father standing proudly next to Magic and Moonshadow. When he was done, he thanked us profusely and added, "That's the first time my kids have ever been impressed by what I do."

Just as we'd planned, we were able to bring Moonshadow and Magic to several hospitals in New York City and along the route home. We were pleased we could visit so many children.

By the time we reached Florida, news hit that the coronavirus we'd heard about was fast-spreading, deadly, and no longer far away but on the move throughout our country as well.

The coronavirus rapidly developed into a global pandemic. To stop the spread, no more large gatherings were being held. Many stores, restaurants, and businesses had to close, and employees worked remotely whenever possible. Many people lost their jobs. We were told to isolate ourselves at home. We felt fortunate that we'd arrived home before the worst of it broke out and everything shut down.

In the days that followed, news channels reported that New York City was the hardest hit area in the country, with a death toll in the thousands. So many people were infected that the medical centers were running out of lifesaving equipment and space. In fact, the Army Corps of Engineers turned the Javits Center, where only weeks earlier we had been attending the toy convention, into a makeshift hospital.

"They're calling New York City the epicenter of the outbreak," Jorge said one evening as we sat down to dinner. "I can't believe we were just there, the streets crowded with people. And now the streets are nearly empty and the hospitals are full. It's shocking."

Schools closed, libraries shut down, and visitors weren't allowed in hospitals. We had to cancel all of our events, and I was sorry so many children would be disappointed. Out in the corral with Jorge one day, I was talking on my cell phone when Magic nudged my arm and seemed to be looking into the screen. That gave me an idea. When I hung up, I said to Jorge, "Remember in New York, when that police officer wanted his children to see him with the horses?"

"Yes, we did FaceTime. His kids were thrilled."

"Right. I'll never forget how excited they were to get a phone call from a horse! I was thinking, what if we did that with children in the hospitals? The ones we can't go to see in person now. We could reach out to them through FaceTime, just like that officer did with his children. That way we could still help while they're unable to get out and we're unable to get in."

Jorge agreed. We set up some bright lights in our living room, groomed Moonshadow, and brought her inside. The first child we called was Sofia, who had been in the hospital for a long time. We arranged the call with a nurse, who answered and got us connected. I heard a voice say, "There's a pony on the phone!"

"What?" she said as the nurse held the phone for her, and then she looked into the screen and said, "Hi!"

"Hi, Sofia," Jorge said. "We're calling from the farm, just checking in to see how you're feeling."

193

Moonshadow looked right into the phone. Most of the horses are good at this because they are used to doing selfies. I think they enjoy seeing their image on the phone screen. Sofia giggled so hard, she couldn't stop. "Hi, horsie!"

"I bet you've never talked to a horse on the phone before," Jorge said.

"I haven't," Sofia said.

"We have a little video to show you." Jorge played a video we'd recorded of the horses running and kicking up their heels in the pasture.

"They're playing." Sofia pointed toward the screen. "Look!"

Jorge read Sofia a short story, spoke a bit longer, and then said goodbye.

"I love you, Moonshadow," Sofia said, flashing a bright smile.

"We miss you," Jorge said. "Goodbye for now."

Every day we spent hours making as many FaceTime calls as possible. We spoke to children who had been isolated because of compromised immune systems, those who were recovering from surgeries, and those alone in hospitals, unable to receive visitors. Every time, no matter their circumstances, the children smiled and laughed when they saw the horses. One little girl giggled as Magic pressed her face close to the camera. "Your nose is so big!" she said. Here was a little girl confined to a bed and hooked up to all kinds of tubes and monitors, yet she was still able to enjoy Magic's antics.

As challenging times continued—longer than we ever expected—some of the temporary changes we were forced to make have become lasting ways of using technology to reach out to people. The FaceTime calls were so successful that we continue to implement them, and we've even found additional uses for FaceTime, such as keeping in touch with children after they've left the hospital. We use Zoom video-conferencing to record a series called "Story Time on the Farm with Mr. Jorge" as a way to help educate and entertain children isolating at home. We pick different horse-themed books we would ordinarily bring to schools and libraries, and we share them with children near and far. The first book we chose was *Sleepy Ponies* by Joy Hicklin. Mercury curled up beside Jorge on the living room sofa. As Jorge read the story, Mercury closed his eyes and drifted off.

"I guess the book lived up to its title," I said. "You put him to sleep."

Thoughts of the residents in the assisted living and memory care facilities we had regularly visited particularly weighed on me, because many of the older adults there weren't experienced with computers. Without visitors and lacking access to social media, they were sure to be isolated and lonely.

We decided to arrange a surprise. We asked the administrators at the facility if they could have the residents line up by their windows. That Sunday we donned face masks and gloves and brought Scout up to the building. We invited a friend to join us—a massive two-thousand-pound Percheron horse named Tiny Prince Charming. Despite their nineteen-hundred-pound weight difference, Scout and Tiny Prince Charming like each other. The bigger horse nuzzled

Scout's nose, as if kissing him. Maintaining proper distance (we jokingly called it "one Percheron length") and wearing masks, we walked the two horses around outside

the building, stopping to peek in at windows and waving signs that said, "We love you." One woman pushed her walker close to the window, stretched out her hand, and began wiggling her fingers. Scout nosed the window. Another woman played a game with Scout, moving her hand across the windowpane and having Scout follow her movements. Each resident was able to make a real, live connection, even through the glass. When we left, everyone at the windows waved goodbye. We couldn't see their smiles behind their masks, but we were sure they were there, just the same as ours.

We did everything we could to stay safe, while safely reaching out to others during the coronavirus crisis. I thought I was handling everything okay, but then the washing machine, television, and my cell phone all broke on the same day. I'd reached my own breaking point. I trudged out to the barn, fighting the negative thoughts crowding my mind. I picked up a brush and figured I'd release my frustration by grooming as many horses as possible. The brisk strokes would feel good to the horses and perhaps quell my pent-up anxiety.

As I brushed, I began thinking about those who were ill and fighting the virus, those who had serious health concerns to worry about, and all the health-care professionals who bravely went to work and were exposed to the virus every day. Our inconveniences were surely mild by comparison. I managed to find numerous silver linings during this time of isolation: slowing down from our hectic schedule of travel and events, finding multiple ways to keep in touch with people even though we couldn't get out, appreciating the things we had, and cherishing our loved ones.

I stepped back and looked at the beautifully groomed horses standing before me, aware that I had one more thing to be grateful for. As I'd smoothed out the tangles from their manes and the coarseness from their coats, I'd smoothed out the rough edges in my thinking as well. The horses would be fine, and so would we. I leaned in close with my head against Magic's neck and gave thanks for the comfort she and the others had brought me that day.

21

"We're all so different, but so much alike."

In all my years working with horses, not a day goes by that I don't learn something. But one of my favorite lessons came recently, from little Mercury and a young Maremma pup named Sirius.

One cool April evening, the air was full of excitement and promise, as a new baby had just come into the world. Jorge patted the sides of the mare and her one-day-old colt, Mercury.

We had just recently added some Maremma pups to the family, too, and they were rolling and playing in one of the stalls. We like to introduce new additions to their environment gradually—first to the sweet, fresh smell of straw on the floor and the playfulness of the sunbeams falling from the rafters. Then to the dusty corral and the swinging gate with its creaky hinges. Later to the pastures and the fields of fresh, green grass. That evening I decided to let the puppies out of the barn one at a time so each of them could see the new colt and so the colt could see the puppies. In our experience it's best to take things slow when helping the animals become acquainted with one another. Bit by bit they see the difference between furry paws and tiny hooves, and they discover the way the puppy's tail wags and the foal's tail swishes. They hear the difference between the dog's woofs and the horse's soft nickers.

Sirius was the first Maremma I let out of the barn. At eight weeks old, he was a typical playful puppy but also tended to be more cautious than the others. Although we named him Sirius after the dog star, the name also fit his serious nature. Sirius is the easiest pup to tell apart from the others too. Most Maremmas are solid white. Sirius's parents and grandparents are all white, and he has five all-white sisters. But Sirius came into the world with black around his eyes, black ears, and a couple large black spots on his sides.

I leaned lightly against a tree in the yard as roly-poly Sirius bounded around on his huge puppy paws. Mercury looked up, cocked his head, and watched Sirius zoom past, then zoom back again. He was clearly taken with this new creature. Mercury's mother grazed nearby. Most mares wouldn't allow a dog anywhere near their newborn foal, but she trusted us, and she also trusted the Maremmas. They help protect the horses, and she considered the dogs part of the herd—even the funny little pint-sized one that bounced about the yard like a jumping bean.

When Sirius finally plopped down in the grass for a rest, Mercury took action. Bounding around on his spindly legs, he set his sights on Sirius and stepped right up to the pup. Mercury lowered his head, Sirius blinked, but neither one budged. They just stayed that way, nose to nose, studying each other. Jorge and I tried not to move a muscle so as not to break the magic, and my heart stirred with happiness. I'd never seen anything like this before.

The two animals remained mesmerized—fuzzy little Mercury and fluffy Sirius. Watching them, I saw that Mercury was only a little larger than the pup. Remarkably, the colt had practically the same markings as the young dog! He was white, with black ears, black on his neck, and a few large black spots on his body. It was almost like looking at twins.

Then Sirius took off, bumble-running around the enclosure again. Mercury followed. Wherever Sirius went, Mercury was right behind. It was adorable watching them run and seeing them gain confidence. Of course, Mercury's legs were longer and more agile than Sirius's, and he galloped around and left poor Sirius in his dust. Each time Mercury ran off, Sirius would follow for a bit, then sit and wait for Mercury to come back and catch up with him. At last, when they were both exhausted, they settled down in the grass and snuggled next to each other for a nap.

From then on, they were always together, running, playing, eating, and sleeping. They even played in the kiddie pool together. Except that Sirius would lie quietly in the pool to cool off, and Mercury would run through it, splash in the water, and run back through the other way! Whenever Jorge would open the door to the pickup truck, they'd both come running and press in against his feet, begging for a ride.

Eventually they both learned to ride in the truck. Each of them is so different—after all, one is a horse and the other is a dog. Yet they are both so much alike.

Horses have to learn many skills in order to be therapy animals, and we work with them step-by-step to teach them what they need to know. But in this case, Sirius also helped teach Mercury. They played chase, which helped the colt learn about having fun. And one day, I watched from the living room window as Sirius sat at the bottom of our porch, contemplating the row of steps before him. Now several months old, he'd seen some of the other puppies—and certainly the older dogs—manage the stairs. All he had to do was give it a try.

Mercury stood there beside him, just watching. It probably hadn't occurred to Mercury to climb the steps, a behavior that comes more naturally for dogs than for horses. Sirius set his oversized front paws on the bottom step and, in his usual slow and steady style, gave it a good think before he proceeded. Then he pulled his chubby body up and paused, looking back as if to say, *See, this is how you do it!* He scrambled up another step, then two more, until he reached the top. He sat there looking at Mercury. *Okay, your turn.*

Mercury tossed his head. Sirius was up there on the porch, and he wasn't. Time to take action. He set a hoof on the first step. Horses don't have good depth perception, and they can

202

be unsure of new surroundings, so I started to move toward the door. But before I could intervene, little Mercury took a step, then another and another, and climbed up to stand on the porch next to his very best friend. They'd worked together and learned all by themselves.

I rarely saw the two of them apart. Watching them play, I wondered if Sirius thought, "I'm a horse!" or if Mercury thought, "I'm a dog!" It didn't matter. The two never wanted to be separated, and they rarely had to be except for when Mercury went off the farm for short training visits.

One morning Jorge and I walked Mercury into the trailer to go to the butterfly garden at the Ronald McDonald House. Sirius jumped and whined to join us. "Sorry, pal, not this time," I said. Sirius barked his disapproval. As we pulled away, I looked back and saw that Sirius had padded over to the front porch and sat solemnly in his new favorite spot at the top of the steps. He sat there and stared at the place where he'd last seen Mercury.

Later, when the truck rattled back up the driveway, I glanced at the porch. There was Sirius still waiting at the top of the steps. He was lying down and rested his head on his paws, but the faithful dog had kept watch until he saw his friend return. At the first glimpse of the truck, Sirius bolted down the steps and ran to greet Mercury, barking for joy. When Jorge opened the trailer gate, the two best friends darted off to the pasture together.

What had caused the dog to wait there so long and keep watch for his friend? How did he know we would return? How could he feel certain that Mercury would be there in the trailer when Jorge opened its gate? Was there some unseen connection that existed between these friends?

The bond between the two moved me so deeply that I began to think about taking the two of them out together. We'd never before brought one of the dogs into a school or library. They were livestock guardian dogs, and that was their job. However, watching the unlikely friends, I kept feeling that they had an important lesson to teach children.

That autumn the two were old enough to make the idea a reality. I decided to start with a daycare I knew of in a nearby inner-city neighborhood. The children there probably didn't receive many surprises, so this seemed like a good place to start.

When we walked in the room, the thirty youngsters were sitting cross-legged on the floor and wriggling with anticipation. "I bet you have a lot in common with your best friends," I said. "You go to the same school. Maybe you like the same toys."

The youngsters nodded.

"But you probably have some differences too. Your hair might be a different color. You live in different homes. You know, we're all so different but so much alike. Now, here is something I bet is the same for all of you . . . do you all like stories?"

"Yes!" they chorused.

"Today I'm going to tell you a story about something that really happened." Then I opened a book I'd written just for the occasion and turned to the first page. "Mercury made his first new friend when he was one day old," I read. "He walked up to Sirius, this fearless little foal, and touched the fluffy puppy on the end of his nose. He knew at once they were so much alike."

"Ahhhh!" the children said. Wonder shone on their faces.

I read about how Mercury loves to run, but Sirius loves to nap on the porch. How Mercury eats hay, but Sirius only likes hay as a soft, comfy place to rest. How Mercury is bold and frisky, but Sirius is shy. Yet they are best friends. "They may be different, but they only see the ways they are alike."

When I finished the book, I smiled and asked, "Is there somebody here you don't know very well?" They all looked around. "Let's say hi to somebody new today."

With the teacher's encouragement, the children looked around and said hi to one another.

"Now, are you ready to meet two new friends?" The children cheered. "Okay, let's all be very quiet. This is something new for them." I pressed a button on my iPod and began the playful music of "The Baby Elephant March" from *The Jungle Book*. Jorge walked in with Mercury on the lead line, and Sirius entered beside them wearing his new bright-red harness and collar. The children all gasped and giggled and pointed, but they did a good job staying quiet—at least as quiet as possible for thirty very excited preschoolers.

Jorge walked the dog and horse around in a circle a few times, and they stayed side by side. "Look, they really are best friends!" exclaimed one little girl.

We talked for a bit, keeping the program short. When we got ready to go, we had everyone line up. As we walked past them to the door, each child had an opportunity to pat or

205

hug Sirius and Mercury. Even the teachers stood in line to have a turn. It showed me how we all have some part of us that can be enriched by the gentle love of animals. And as each child and adult hugged Mercury and Sirius, I silently wished that these unlikely friends would give that person exactly what they needed in that moment. The smiles on their faces as each one released their embrace helped me believe that would come true.

Before we walked out the door, Jorge reminded the group, "Mercury and Sirius say, just because we're different doesn't mean we can't be friends."

When we got back to the farm, I let Sirius out of the truck, and Jorge opened the door of the trailer and led Mercury down the ramp. The two ran off to join the others out in the pasture. Jorge put his arm around my shoulders. "They did so well for their first time out. I hope the children will remember this day." I nodded, yet felt my thoughts press in even deeper. Some of those children lived in a tough neighborhood. Some had difficult home lives. Who knew what obstacles they faced each day or would be confronted with in the future? They'd have to find some strength within themselves to do the right things. What if a few moments with Sirius and Mercury reminded them to be kind? To accept each other? To love one another? To know that they are loved? What if the seeds of that strength began in just that moment? Maybe that twinkling of time was what it took to propel them forward to greater things.

None of us are immune to life's challenges. I've had my share. There have been times when I didn't feel loved and times when I've felt alone. I've made mistakes. I've neglected things I should have done. I've tried to do valiant things

206

that didn't work out. I've had trauma and pain. My life isn't necessarily what I'd planned. But I know there's hope because I've seen it. No matter how challenging or difficult or desperate someone's life may be, when the horses come in, that person responds. I've never seen it fail. They sit up, they perk up, they smile, they laugh. Sometimes they cry.

So many times we are inserted into someone's life for just a brief time. A moment in a hospital. A moment at a school. Maybe an ordinary moment, or maybe the worst moment of a person's life. And that person watches the horses walk in with their cloppety hooves, and they clasp their arms around a soft, furry neck, and they sense the animal move in closer, and they feel the warmth, and it's good. Maybe they've almost given up, but in that moment they feel compelled to reach forward to another moment, and maybe that moment isn't so bad. And that's when hope emerges. As we get older, we don't remember the days; we remember the moments. And I dream of continuing to be where I can help whenever the need arises, whatever the moment.

Jorge went back to work in the barn, and I wandered out to the pasture. As I made a crooked path through the stubbly grass, some of the horses trotted up to me one by one and in nosy groups. Magic, Sweetheart, Scout, Dream. They said hello, reaching out to me with a gentle nuzzle. I watched others grazing in the distance. Anthem, Prince, Sparkle, Toby.

The day began to fade, casting rosy-pink hues across the sky. The little herd wandered toward the inner pasture, where they'd be safely enclosed for the night. A wisp of a breeze brushed against my cheek as I returned to the barn. I leaned against the fence just outside the doors, watching the horses amble toward me. They returned from the outer pasture without coaxing every evening, trusting they were headed someplace warm and safe. They didn't have to fear the future. They relied on some mysterious equine hope that we would always be there for them the next day, the next night. I felt sure it was what Sirius must have felt that time he sat on the top step and waited for his best friend to return, without any certainty that the trailer would ever reappear. He kept watch because he had hope.

The horses came to me, their tails swaying like gentle pendulums. They slowly trotted through the gate near where I stood, brushing against my leg and acknowledging me with a friendly nicker. Each one had ministered to me throughout the years. Each one had filled me with comfort and peace when times were rough. I captured the moment in my mind, with the little herd all around me. And in that precious moment, I clearly saw that no matter the challenges, my hope for tomorrow is always just a hoofbeat away.

Frequently Asked Questions

1. How long does it take to train a therapy horse?

Every horse is different. All of our therapy horses go through about a two-year basic training program, including hospital work. They are always practicing and learning new skills. It takes a lot of work to make what they do seem effortless. It also helps that our foals start hospital training visits at a young age alongside their therapy horse mothers.

2. Can a miniature horse live in my house with me?

Our therapy horses work indoors, but we would never make them live indoors. They may be small, but they are horses in every way. They need a lot of exercise to stay healthy and happy. In the wild, horses move ten to twenty miles a day. Movement keeps their hooves flexing and blood circulating.

As herd animals they should have the companionship of other horses. It would be stressful for a miniature horse to live by itself, especially in a small place. Even though they do unusual work, we want them to live natural lives. Their needs and happiness are the most important thing to us.

3. Do all miniature horses make good therapy horses?

All horses of any breed have different personalities. It takes a very special horse to be both safe and happy working indoors in challenging situations like hospitals. Miniature horses can do many wonderful things. It is a matter of matching the right horse to the right job.

4. Can I buy one of your horses?

Gentle Carousel does not sell horses. A foal is only born if we are adding a future therapy horse to the program. If you are looking for a miniature horse as a pet, we always encourage our friends to contact local horse rescues. Horses are herd animals and would be very unhappy alone, so if you are looking to rescue a miniature horse, make sure you can take care of at least two.

5. Do your horses enjoy what they do?

We would never make a horse work if they did not enjoy what they do and the attention they receive.

Each individual therapy horse works no more than two days a week, unless they are traveling. They spend the rest of their time living a very natural life with a herd of lifelong equine friends. We want them to be excited about going out to meet people and happy when the herd comes to greet them when they return home.

6. How long do miniature horses live?

Healthy and well-cared-for miniature horses often live longer on average than full-sized horse breeds. The average life span of a miniature horse is twenty-five to thirty-five years.

7. Do Maremma dogs make good pets?

Maremma sheepdogs are a breed of dog that needs a job to do to be happy. They also need space to run and a caregiver who understands them. The Maremma Sheepdog Club of America does not recommend the Maremma as a pet. They are an independent working dog with two thousand years of genetic history for livestock guardianship. Our Maremma sheepdogs all have different personalities, but they all love spending time with the therapy horses.

8. How can I contact or support the work of Gentle Carousel Miniature Horses?

You can find contact information, donate, or learn ways to follow the horses by visiting our website at gentlecarouseltherapyhorses.com. You can also keep up-to-date with happenings on the farm with our weekly digest, and follow us on social media at www .facebook.com/TherapyHorses and www.instagram .com/gentlecarousel.

Magic the Hero Horse's Awards

One of History's 10 Most Heroic Animals—*Time* magazine

Most Heroic Pet in America—AARP

A *Reader's Digest* / AmericanTowns Power of 1 Hero

One of the 10 Most Heroic Animals of 2010—*Newsweek* / *Daily Beast*

2014 E.T. York Distinguished Service Award

One of Seven Most Notable Animal Heroes in the World—*Daily Mirror* 2014

Honorary Deputy with the Alachua County Sheriff's Office

Certificate of Special Congressional Recognition

Autism Paws of Honor Award

Pet Hero of the Year 2016 / Florida Veterinary Medical Association Hall of Fame

American Red Cross A Hero Among Us Outstanding
Service Award—2016

Ronald McDonald House Caring and Sharing
Award—2017

United States Equestrian Federation / EQUUS Foundation
Horse Stars Hall of Fame

Haven Hospice Volunteer of the Year Service
Award—2019

Breyer Portrait Model Horse

Acknowledgments

Thank you to all of the amazing volunteers who have helped Gentle Carousel Miniature Therapy Horses through the years, and to the wonderful animals who have touched my life, especially the loving horses of Gentle Carousel. Thank you to everyone who has played a part in making this book a reality, including Peggy for all your support and patience, and to Jorge, who brings so much goodness into the world every day.

—Debbie

Thank you to Debbie for Monday mornings at 10:30, and to Debbie and Jorge for being willing to share your story, and to all the wonderful miniature horses who make so many people happy. With much appreciation to Rachelle Gardner for believing in us, to Vicki Crumpton for her vision and support, and to all the great folks at Revell. A special thank-you to Mike for your constant loving support, and to my faithful friend and ever-helpful critiquer, Susan Karas.

—Peggy

Debbie Garcia-Bengochea and her husband, Jorge, co-founded Gentle Carousel Miniature Therapy Horses, one of the largest equine therapy programs in the world. Their teams of tiny horses bring love to more than twenty-five thousand adults and children each year inside hospitals, hospice programs, and assisted living facilities, and to those who have experienced traumatic events. The multiple-award-winning charity is celebrating over twenty years of service.

Debbie is a former teacher and elementary school principal and an award-winning commercial artist and photographer. As the education director for Gentle Carousel, Debbie created Reading Is Magic, a literacy program to encourage young and at-risk readers, and has written a children's book, *Mercury and Sirius*. Connect with Debbie at gentlecarousel therapyhorses.com, on Facebook at www.facebook.com /TherapyHorses, and on Instagram @gentlecarousel.

Peggy Frezon is a contributing editor of *All Creatures* magazine and has been a regular writer for *Guideposts* magazine for nearly twenty years. She's an award-winning author of books about the human-animal bond, including *The Dog in the Dentist Chair . . . and Other True Stories about Animals Who Help, Comfort, and Love Kids* (Paraclete Press, 2019) and *Faithfully Yours: The Amazing Bond between Us* *and the Animals We Love* (Paraclete Press, 2015). Her work can also be found in *All God's Creatures Daily Devotionals* (Guideposts Books) and *One Minute Devotionals* (Guideposts Books) and dozens of *Chicken Soup for the Soul* books. Peggy and her husband rescue senior golden retrievers and volunteer doing therapy dog work. In addition to working at nursing homes and colleges, their twelve-year-old rescue golden retriever is a book buddy for a first-grade class. They currently share their home with goldens Ernest and Pete. Connect with Peggy at www.peggyfrezon.com, on Facebook at www.facebook.com/PeggyFrezonBooks, and on Instagram @pfrezon.